Vermont Diary

DATE DUE

DEMCO 38-297

Teachers&Writers
84 Fifth Avenue, New York, New York 10011

ISBN 0-915924-07-2

This book is made possible by a grant from the National Endowment for the Arts in Washington D.C., a federal agency.

Library of Congress Cataloging in Publication Data

Hoffman, Marvin, 1939-
    Vermont diary.

1. Language arts (Elementary).   2. Open plan schools. I. Title.
LB1576.H613   372.6'044   78-16429
ISBN 0-915924-07-2

Table of Contents

INTRODUCTION

Before beginning to write on this snowy New Hampshire morning, I sat by the fire with a tastefully done collection of essays by poets who have taught in the schools. A little scared, I suppose, I was looking for a starting place. It's been two and a half years since I left my own classroom and four and a half years from the time I gave up the directorship of Teachers & Writers Collaborative. My work with children and, later, with teachers and teaching interns during these years has kept me from writing, and I feared that "the thrill was gone," that what I wanted to say about teaching and writing had faded.

But the poets' essays turn me back to the central thread of my experience. What they have written is full of good ideas and fine techniques; still, reading them I am seized with the anxiety I feel in facing a book of jokes or riddles. Will I remember a single one to repeat to my children? Desperately, I grasp for some organizing principle, some mnemonic to prevent a complete rout. But it's no use because in the end my way of learning is no different from that of most children: without a context, without a concrete relationship to a particular person or group, without a vision of a particular physical space, these ideas are without life. Where are the children hiding among all these techniques? And where are the teachers?

I realize that in my contributions to the *Whole Word Catalogue* and to the Teachers & Writers Collaborative (T & W) Newsletters, I have been guilty of the same kind of intimidation of my teacher-readers who may have found themselves paralyzed amnesiacs during their classroom writing periods— unless perhaps they thought of a particular child or a particular space in their classroom as they read of one or another approach to language. Now that I've passed through the transformation from writer-in-the-schools (I am not, in fact, a writer) to classroom teacher, I have a message in several parts to relay: 1) Thank you, and thank you again, to the writers at T & W who helped me and so many other teachers and writers to find a way to begin to write with children, a way that did not dilute the pleasure of words and language. 2) It is, nevertheless, *different* for a classroom teacher who must learn to live with his/her children through rather lean times and must carry a responsibility for a range of learning that goes well beyond creative writing. 3) Despite the additional burdens that come with the relinquishing of the poets' charismatic cloak for the smock of day-to-day contact, it is possible, perhaps *more* possible, for a classroom teacher to develop a writing program in which the work is richer and even more prolific than what is elicited by the specialist. 4) Maybe writers-in-the-schools need to look at new roles which they can play in the education of children.

Many writers come to see the inherent limitations of their roles after the initial delight of discovering that they *can* talk to children, that the spitballs and thumbtacks of disrespect are rare, and that most children *are* responsive to interesting ideas, energetically presented. The Teachers & Writers Collaborative staff has taken the lead in moving toward more and more intensive and organic relationships with specific schools and classrooms: from one-shot visits; to one-day-per-week classroom visits over blocks of time (ten weeks, one semester, one year, multi-year periods); to even more intensive, semipermanent presences of *teams* of specialists such as the one Phillip Lopate described so effectively in *Being With Children*. All these still fall short. Change and all its confusing complexities occur or fail to occur in the classroom, and one must be there to see it through. The visiting poet routine has been extremely effective, but it will reach its saturation point soon and will go the way of the dinosaurs unless a new reason for being can be formulated. It may be best for writers to concentrate on teacher-training or to serve as advisors or directors of curriculum development teams made up primarily of teachers.

That uncovering of new roles for writers is an issue they will have to explore for themselves. I have different business here, namely to tell you about a writing program that was conducted without benefit of writers in a "regular classroom," and was overseen only by the regular classroom teachers. Any change that is dependent on superhuman, charismatic visitors only serves to confirm ordinary mortals in their belief that they are not brilliant enough to pull off such a coup. "Why bother?" is their understandable reaction, but it need not be the inevitable one.

Chapter 1

THE ROAD TO FAIRLEE

My professional life is full of the twists and turns that at certain times display an extraordinary inner logic and at others seem like random paths through a maze with no exit. I was trained as a clinical psychologist and after finishing graduate school went to Mississippi in 1965 to teach at a black college. This was meant to be my modest contribution to the "Movement," though the college turned out to be even more timid than my wife and I, and we were soon searching for a larger form of engagement. I became one of the central staff members of what was probably the first large-scale Headstart Program in the U.S. in those earliest days (1966) of the War on Poverty. Although I learned a lot more about young children than I had ever known before, they were not my immediate responsibility. I was in charge of the community organizers, the health and dental programs—all those larger nonclassroom concerns that we knew would make a major difference in the lives of children. For this realization and for its absolute commitment to community control of institutions, the program—The Child Development Group of Mississippi—will undoubtedly earn itself a long footnote in the social and political history of the '60s.

When I left, in January 1968, to go back where I thought I belonged —Brooklyn—it was with some sense that the role of white folks had changed in a predominantly black organization. Moreover, we were weary from the unending political battles with Mississippi politicians and Washington bureaucrats, which placed us permanently on the edge of annihilation.

In New York we found ourselves in the midst of the New York teachers strike (1968) and the struggle for community control that had precipitated it. We thought we had seen how well community control could work and threw our energies into support of its proponents. The sourness of that experience hardly needs to be retold. Suffice it to say that it would be hard to find a single child in New York whose education has been measurably improved by this battle. I was disenchanted with the politics of education and wished more than anything to become involved in the *substance* of education. What was it we were fighting for anyway?

7

Teachers & Writers Collaborative was so attractive to me precisely because it had a specific focus, its people were in direct contact with children, and it was free of smothering political entanglements. Besides, my wife was a writer. I knew a fair bit about writing and writers, had a romantic respect for them—collectively—and had an amused tolerance of their less stellar individual qualities. During my two years (1969-1971) as director of the Collaborative, I visited a lot of classrooms; talked endlessly with some intelligent, committed writers about teaching and children; oversaw the publication of a lot of material (which I still take a secret, subversive pleasure in discovering on classroom shelves in the most unlikely places); and did a lot of tiresome, dreary check signing, fund-raising, and proposal writing.

I was increasingly more jealous of the writers. They were doing the real thing, working their magic with the kids, while I was a grey "facilitator," making it all possible but never "making" it. Dick Murphy,* the associate director at T & W, felt the same restlessness and had found a classroom in which to try out some of his ideas. These experiments later became the "Imaginary Worlds" project.

My chance came from an unexpected direction. I had written a review of a lovely book called *Homework* by Gloria Channon, a seasoned teacher in East Harlem who had recorded the pain of sloughing off a traditional style of teaching in favor of something more in keeping with the needs of individual children. Gloria called to thank me for the review, and I soon found myself arranging a weekly schedule of visits to her classroom (Who me? I'm only a poor administrator!).

I came each week bearing the assortment of writing ideas I had picked up from my colleagues at T & W, as well as some materials with

---

*Dick is one of the most well-educated and well-read college dropouts I have ever met. Some people fail school, but school failed Dick. After an unhappy time at Oberlin and New York University, Dick went to Mississippi in 1962 to work with the *Mississippi Free Press,* a newspaper which was one of the early outgrowths of the civil rights movement. In 1965 he too went to work for the Child Development Group of Mississippi where he was responsible for the production of instructional materials for parents and staff of limited educational background. This was an outgrowth of an adult literacy project he had also worked on in Mississippi.

Dick moved to New York in late 1967, where he and Sheila helped found a company that was producing materials for one of the major textbook publishers, a venture which was as unprofitable for the soul as it was profitable for the bank account. We came to T & W together in September, 1969. Dick's primary responsibilities were for publications, especially the newsletter. Our decision to leave T & W for Vermont was a collective one, and grew out of a shared sense that we wanted direct contact with children and an opportunity to develop our ideas about writing.

When we left Vermont, Dick went on to head the School Around Us in Kennebunk, Maine.

which one could make words in physically interesting ways—Dymo label-makers, colored carbon paper, apparatus for doing invisible writing. It was a liberating but disquieting experience. How shocked I was to see what a messy, disorganized classroom Gloria seemed to run and how little interesting material there was for the children to work with. Yet, Gloria had a relationship with these youngsters that even allowed for high-pitched parental anger, the kind that does no harm because there is no hatred in it, only frustrated concern.

In what must be the closest male analogue to the maternal instinct, I knew that I wanted a group of my own kids. I wanted to understand their lives, know their brothers and sisters, really make a difference in reshaping the contours of their lives in a way that an hour a week with a Dymo label-maker would never allow. This messianic madness could only be realized for me in a small, manageable-sized situation, one in which I could see and hold all the pieces. No more dealing with twenty different schools, each with 1,500 kids who disappeared into the maw of the city at three o'clock.

So Dick and Sheila Murphy (who with me constituted just about the entire central operation of T & W), my wife, and I set about looking for a place that would take us in:

> The four of us who are making this proposal have worked together for three years, first with the Child Development Group of Mississippi, a state-wide Headstart Project, and later with Teachers and Writers Collaborative in New York City. Although we have varied experience in many kinds of teaching, we feel that our involvement in educational change has been too theoretical. We have never had an opportunity to apply ourselves to and to learn from practical day to day work in a school of our own. We are afraid of the ease with which one can generalize from inexperience; the more you don't know, the more you theorize. We would like to combine our strengths and begin, within a sympathetic public system, a Resource Center for teachers interested in learning more about the atmosphere, pedagogy, and tools of open education.
>
> From our past experience we have learned the futility and bitterness of establishing another, and then another, institution outside the moribund system. Public schooling is a monster that may one day be subdued by the righteous, but we have grown weary of fighting in the manner of saints. We have come late to the realization that while "the system" may be a monster, there are people within that system who are all too willing to change if they can only find support. It is to those people that we would like to bring our ideas, and from them that we would like to learn. In short, we want to avoid at all cost establishing another alternative which, by becoming a parochial success, strikes another blow at the public schools where most of our children are and will continue to be.

We have permitted ourselves the luxury of looking for a school community with the right combination of enthusiasm for change but skepticism about alternatives merely for the sake of something different; of respect for children, teachers and parents; of support for traditional teachers, some of whom were superlative teachers long before the gurus identified what was "inherently" wrong with their method; of courage to abandon myths about professional dignity, authority, and expertise.

From: *An Alternative School Proposal*
by Sheila Murphy

It was a time when so many white people were running *from* the city, the war, the blacks, and the "system," and I have no doubt that there was an element of flight in our decision as well. But we were also running *to* something more positive—a deep immersion in the lives of real children on a small enough scale to keep that engagement human. I've been in the middle of one too many grand-scale and grandiose ventures that touch no one and harm a few. There is nothing that I believe in with such absolute conviction as what the *I Ching* calls "the redeeming power of the small."

Through an acquaintance who was already living in Vermont, we spoke with a superintendent who appeared to understand what we were after and proposed that we establish ourselves in the Fairlee Elementary School, where there was a kindergarten in need of staff and a large unused space capable of housing a Resource Center. The kindergarten, with eighteen children, was privately supported. It rented a classroom in the public school and functioned as if it were part of the school. The parent group that supported the kindergarten hired Sheila Murphy as their teacher. Dick Murphy, Rosellen and I took turns serving as her aide in the mornings, as much for what we could learn from her as to be of use. The school had about eighty students, grades one through eight, with whom we worked in groups of ten or so, once or twice a week. The parent tuitions for the kindergarten plus a generous gift from the Lebensburger Fund were our sources of support that first year.

10

Chapter 2

THE SETTING

I could tell you about my memories of the seasons that shift as spectacularly here as any place I've ever lived—from heat and thick river fog; to autumnal color; to the beautiful snow, free of the sullying New York footprints; to the green return, particularly to the little patch of land we have marked off as our garden. I could tell you how the seasons are delineated in my mind as reigns of various bug dynasties. When we arrived in September, the room that was to become the Resource Center was literally crawling with crickets, a rather incongruous sight against the wall-to-wall carpeting. They were followed by the house flies that multiplied in the kindergarten and in our apartment farther into the winter than I ever dreamed possible. The shortest reign of all was the one-night stand of the glowworms whose eerie emanations we saw along the side of the road at the end of a late-night walk in April. When we returned the next night for another look, they were gone. Then we were into the "black fly" season about which we had been warned. The warnings seemed laughable when we discovered that black flies were not the mammoth house flies we had envisioned, but tiny aphidlike (perhaps they are aphids, for all I know) creatures who proved less than amusing as they ate big hunks out of us, our children, and our garden. Now there are the mosquitoes, and I've begun to see crickets in among our vegetables, so we'll soon be ready for another turn of the wheel.

Or I could tell you about the beautiful cliff side that runs up behind the school. In past years they tell us that from the classroom windows you could see herds of deer grazing on the mountainside, and the kids often climb up the power line cut to look for the tracks of the bear family that lives up top—if the hunters didn't get them last season.

Despite the fact that everything I've described so far represents one real face of Fairlee and our experiences in and around it, the truth is that, on balance, Fairlee is a very unromantic place. The school is unspeakably characterless, if not ugly. Friends and family who see our four-square cinder block nonentity are visibly disappointed, robbed of their visions of a rustic one-room schoolhouse. The rooms are strung out as in a railroad shack or, better, as in one of those busy doctor's offices where you're herded into one of many examining rooms that are designed to minimize possible contacts with the other patients. The gym occupies a far larger percentage of the school space than the classrooms: a sign, we thought at once, of what the local priorities are. In fact, the space also turns out to be a godsend during the cold and miserable winter when the children are trapped inside for days on end.

The town itself has even less to wax rhapsodic about. The main street is a combination of superfluous gas stations, somewhat neglected old houses, and unattractive stores, plus one diner-truck stop that services the commercial traffic moving on or off the interstate highway that begins (ends) in Fairlee—for the moment. (NOTE: The next year another six-mile stretch was opened, taking the traffic past Fairlee, straight north, enroute to Canada. The ribbon of traffic now unwinds directly behind the school, ending the redeeming link between the school grounds and the cliff side.)

The town is rather compact, unlike many others in the area, which tend to sprawl over miles of back roads. Fairlee is squeezed between the cliffs and the river so those people who don't live right "in town" are on the farms, some active and some unworked, on the old highway north or south of town; or in among the summer houses and tourist facilities that surround Lake Morey (the town's one and only income-producing resource); or in one of several semisuburban subdevelopments, which contain the kind of ticky-tacky houses that, to the American yeoman, represent a badge of success.

Although there are many people we've come to respect and admire —more later about them—I don't think it's unfair to say that on the whole the people seem to lack a certain essential vitality and vividness. The ghost of Mississippi hovers over us all, serving as the standard against which we seem to measure all our subsequent experiences. The vibrant speech, the music, the people rooted in a place that has enriched their spirits while it starved their bodies—all these find few parallels in Northern New England. Here there are only scattered vestiges of local culture—the traditions of maple sugaring, town meeting, the Yankee speech, the tall tales of hard winters, the Anglo-Scottish ethnic heritage. What remains of these has been packaged for the tourist trade, an unmistakeable sign that they are no longer viable. It's all been traded in for the same television-consumer culture that has sapped the rest of the country of so much of *its* vitality. Kids and adults are more linked in their psyches to the Partridge Family, Archie Bunker and "Laugh-In" than to the

12

Green Mountain Boys or Samuel Morey.* The prevailing obsessions are with snowmobiles, camp trailers, high-powered rifles, and color television sets. There's plenty of hidden poverty, but for the most part there's an air of rather untroubled satisfaction. There are personal and communal *annoyances* rather than PROBLEMS to be struggled with: none of the strains that can, at times, bring out the larger-than-life qualities of heroism or villainy in New York or Mississippi or a dozen other more rough-edged places. Struggles with people and about ideas *seem* to have been displaced by the struggle with the elements. The extraordinary homogeneity of the population accounts for a lot of the flat, worked-out quality of the people and institutions—no injections of different values, life styles, and traditions that provide a kind of hybrid vigor to more cosmopolitan places. Not only are there no blacks, Jews, or Orientals, but there are few nationalities other than the "Anglos." Several months ago we drove to Barre, a granite-quarrying town about thirty miles from here, and we could immediately sense a kind of bustle and vitality that I think is attributable to the large Italian population that had been drawn there by the stone-cutting work in the quarries. It was precisely what is missing in Fairlee and environs.

Somehow homogeneity, insularity, conservatism, and intolerance seem to go together and feed on one another. Outsiders, particularly those who can be subsumed under the vague heading of "hippies," become the repository of so many buried fantasies and fears. As lightly as we have trod through the year, I'm sure that we are, above all, New Yorkers, long-hairs, Jews (some of us), and braless (?!) in the minds of many local folk.

Sadly, almost everyone in the local population has one or more such stigmas to carry and finds himself almost as far outside the mainstream as we are. They may be Catholic, Irish, part-Italian, New Yorkers or New Jerseyites of too recent vintage, have aesthetic interests, dislike snowmobiles, or any combination of the above. This is what makes stereotyping unproductive, and ironically it is also one of the things that made our presence politically tenable and many of the social relationships with parents and other townspeople cordial and at times friendly. There were enough clusters of people around who were eagerly looking for something different for their children than what was already being offered or were at least tolerant of a style of activity that didn't seem unduly harebrained.

---

*A local inventor of considerable genius who was supposedly cheated out of credit for the steamboat by Robert Fulton.

I don't know how to convey our sense of this complexity within the relative homogeneity. It has been the most sobering revelation about Fairlee and undoubtedly about any place one looks at and lives with for more than an overnight stay. So much of the broad generalizing I've done about the town is not drastically different from what I might have said after a month in the area. True, Fairlee is a blue collar, lower middle-class community where middle-class aspirations and styles hold sway. But it's no less true that different families have made that middle-class life style serve very different ends, particularly in the kind of children the families have chosen to rear. There are children as mean-spirited, intolerant, acquisitive, and materialistic as my most deep-seated anti-middle-class prejudices might have conjured up. Yet there are also families in which the children have been encouraged to indulge their curiosity, to develop a kind of gentle humanity, and to achieve a kind of self-sufficiency that is born more of a pleasure at mastery than of defensive self-protection. I am tempted to offer a dozen cases in point here, which is perhaps the only way to drive off the stereotypes, but I know I will lose myself in them. Perhaps after the rest of the story is told.

When Bob Sheridan, the district superintendent, first showed us the room that was to be the Resource Center, I was overwhelmed by the amount of space we were going to be permitted to lay claim to. The room, more than a double classroom in size, was part of an addition that had been built onto the school in anticipation of an increase in the town's population resulting from the impending extension of the interstate to Fairlee. It was one of the rare occasions on which a small, tight-fisted community had planned anything with an eye to the future. Inevitably it all worked out wrong, as the path of the interstate cut its way through a residential area with a large number of school-age children. The net result was a decline in the student body and one oversize albatross, which contained nothing but a set of movable book wagons bought from the local office supply company. Collectively they were known as the school library.

When we actually sat down to plan out what we wanted to do with all that space, it began to appear like something less than an undiluted blessing. Cinder block walls on which little could be hung, ugly wall-to-wall carpeting of the indoor-outdoor variety, institutional yellow paint on the walls, only one bank of windows along a small part of one wall, and three unbroken rows of fluorescent fixtures that emitted an incessant drone of the kind first designed to break political prisoners during the Moscow Purge Trials. No nooks and crannies, no textures, no color. And everywhere the specter of one great stain of paint, printer's ink, developing chemicals, and food coloring creeping across the rug, engulfing everything. (Not a far cry from what actually came to pass.)

Thus began our magnificent obsession with space, a year-long orgy of drawing plans, building, moving, tearing down, rebuilding, cleaning, and still more diagramming. By the end of the year we had something that was more or less livable but still very unsatisfactory. The importance of spatial arrangements, layout of materials, definition of areas is one of those issues that all of us were already attuned to in the abstract, but the difficulty of translating that into a concrete reality is something else again.

At the outset the task was especially complicated because we didn't have a very clear idea of what was going to be happening in that room. There was no specific program to be carried out there and no particular group of kids who would be living in that room. In a very real sense the designing and building for the Resource Center *was* our program for the first month or so. And that turned out to be a good thing in many ways. The seventh and eighth graders whose classroom connected with the Resource Center were almost always at loose ends because their teacher, who was also the principal, fancied himself an open-classroom practitioner. (READ: Let the kids do what they want; I can't be bothered.) So when the saws, the drills, the wood, and nails began appearing in the Resource Center, we were the only show in town for the boys in that class. (The girls kept their distance for a good long time. It was months before I could identify them by name.) And some of those boys who never would have responded to our more cerebral approaches and activities were in there with us all the time, sometimes to our chagrin. Their energy was rarely balanced with forethought or precision. They measured inaccurately, cut unevenly, and hammered in ten unsightly nails where only two were needed.

Even at that, some of them were vastly better carpenters than we were. Whatever one might say about the plastic world they aspired to or were already living in, it is also true that their world abounded in more practical knowledge than mine had. They had seen their fathers put up houses or additions or hunting cabins; they were more likely to know the difference between a mole and a woodchuck, or how a cow was made to yield continuous milk; they knew the difference between a differential and a distributor. My growing-up world seemed so much more ethereal than theirs. I never learned how to *do* anything, was given the impression that there was something sullying about even wanting to know such things. This, however, was the domain of the hewers of wood and drawers of water.

Again I don't want to romanticize what these kids had and what I didn't. They were unquestionably more crippled by the imbalance between the practical and the "intellectual" than I was. I'm only saying that there's something unnatural about being taught to hover above the earth with your super-charged jet-pack of hot air without ever putting your feet solidly on the earth. There's so much you don't see, so many of the basic building blocks that are missing. Consider the mortification, for example, of facing the task of building a simple 5' x 5' x 5' cube to serve as a typing cubicle below and a study platform above and realizing that you have not the slightest idea of how to make such a body stand erect and rigid. Never to have *seen* what keeps houses from falling down or swaying!

I think this is an important point to look at closely because, in miniature, it is the problem that many aspiring open-classroom teachers have. What do you do if you were the kind of kid who was brought up on an exclusive diet of books, with essentially no hobbies, without the chance to explore the natural world, and if your later education and adult life has done nothing to change that. Suddenly you have chosen to place yourself into a relationship with kids that casts you in the role of jack-of-all-trades, knowledgeable in everything from carpentry to birds because you believe that kids learn best by doing, by wrestling with the concrete problems that present themselves through the handling of materials. Add to that the problem of not being gifted manually in a way that makes any craft natural to you, and you have a complete blueprint for a career in which aspirations rooted in certain ideological beliefs clash directly with your abilities to act on them.

But persistence sometimes compensates for the lack of other gifts, and we learned over the year to become less incompetent carpenters, modest photographers, and novice bookbinders, proving that our educational philosophy holds for teachers, if not always for students. I feel as if there were so many simple things I've learned to do during these years, so many things that were previously inaccessible to me.

What we emerged with after our first round of building was a stage in one corner, made of movable triangular and square sections that fit together jigsaw-fashion to form a large triangular stage surface; a darkroom of plywood and heavy cardboard carved out of another corner of the room adjacent to the sink counter; the two-tiered study and typing platform mentioned before. No sooner was it in place against the wall than a half-dozen sizable eighth graders clambered up the ladder and stretched out full-length on the upper desk with hardly a quiver in the braces. Joy!

16

Finally our most outrageous and nonfunctional construction occupied the center of the room and became our greatest conversation piece. We went to the blacksmith and had him bend a long metal rod into a giant hoop five or six feet in diameter. From this hoop we hung colored netting, the kind that bridesmaids might use, and the whole construction was hung from the ceiling, marking off a large cylindrical space. We called it the magic circle, but the kids were convinced that we were constructing a shower in the Resource Center. Kids did come to sit inside it from time to time, but the truth is that it didn't serve any purpose other than to fill some of that ugly space with something to snag the eye and to set a tone for what could go on in the Resource Center, as opposed to other, saner realms. I think it served that purpose admirably well, and later, when we were thoroughly sick of it and when the program had a more substantial basis for its identity, we took it down and stashed it away.

All these efforts consumed the better part of a month, and still the room was only a bit less cavernous and uninviting than when we had begun. We had to face up to the fact that if we waited until the room satisfied our tastes before starting our regular activities, the year could trickle away with nothing to show for it. I was very aware of the fact that I was *afraid* to start. I had deep doubts about what I was really capable of on my own, in direct contact with a group of kids. After all that preaching about education and change, all the facile criticisms of what other people were writing about and doing in education, what if I fell flat on my face? What if the kids hated me? What if I had no ideas?

It's a gloomy, early winter afternoon. A large number of kids have stayed after school to "work" in the Resource Center. Five or six of the third graders have spent every available minute, since they deposited their coats and lunch boxes on the floor, playing hide-and-seek among the bookcases. Two boys are at the printing press printing endless copies of *Go Artic-Cat, Rupp 400,* and other soul-stirring snowmobile slogans on the press, stacking the copies one on top of another to smudge. I know they will leave them behind in any case when they depart at the end of the day. Ricky and Cliff are in the darkroom making unclear prints from a set of scratched negatives that one of the other kids left lying on the counter at the end of the day. Darlene and Cindy have commandeered the tape recorder and have moved it up to the platform where they are taking turns compiling the honor roll of who loves (hates) whom in their fifth-grade class. Posey (my wife) is onstage with a group of kids who have trapped her into directing a play, which consists of people sitting around in a cafe drinking beer as they watch a chorus line of go-go dancers. I know she is agonizing over how to turn this melee into some kind of creative activity, particularly as we face the imminent arrival and critical eye of the parents who pick their kids up at five o'clock on Resource Center days. Dick has made the same choice of moving off to a corner with one kid who is eager to finish the play he is working on. But I am feeling completely powerless to stand in the face of the galloping chaos. I have retreated to my own corner near the hall door, the farthest possible point from the various clusters of children, and have sat down on the floor with my back against the wall. From time to time a student approaches, heading for the hall. I glare at him, tell him he can't go out because the janitor is cleaning the hall and I've already had two arguments with him about people stepping in his sweeping compound. I hate the children and myself and stare off into space wondering how I ever came to be in this godforsaken place and what ever made me succumb to the delusion that I wanted to—could—work with children.

That was a real afternoon in the Resource Center, the fulfillment of my darkest visions of what could go wrong. But it was, blessedly, a rarer occurrence than I feared it might be in those first moments of paralysis prior to taking the plunge. All that insecurity coupled with the guilt of financing the potential disaster with money from friends who trusted us more than we trusted ourselves.

The students in grades three through eight were divided into groups of eight to ten each and were scheduled for from one hour to one and a half hours each week in the Resource Center. The circumscribed time periods with each group were a disappointment to us, more fragmented than we had hoped. But the kids were shuffled around in the course of a week between phys. ed., art, music, special reading, ski instruction, and any number of other "special" activities, and their schedule could bear no more.

The first weeks and months of actual work with the kids were a quick playback of the themes that had evolved during our time at Teachers and Writers. We had been billed as specialists in children's writing, and despite the fact that we didn't want to be trapped by that narrow definition of what we hoped to do, we needed some quick and visible successes, in the manner of community organizers, to establish ourselves. We went through the whole cycle of writing about "wishes, lies, and dreams." Both the derivative nature of the ideas and the quality of kids' responses to them left me feeling very uneasy. What the kids had to say was so bland and, for the most part, predictable. All the fire, the dramatic flair that we remembered (or seemed to remember) from the writings of kids in the city was strangely absent. The extravagantly fantastic and the sordidly sociological gave way to snowmobiles, hunting, falling off horses, and the like. What the kids had to say about the natural world reflected little sense of mystery and wonder. Instead there was a cruel, unfeeling attitude toward animals and wildlife that made us wonder whether our own attitudes on the subject were hopelessly romantic intellectualizations from the heads of city folk who were viewing the natural world from a distance.

I am making a deliberate effort to reach back into that early part of the first year to reconstruct what we thought of the kids' work then because our assessment of it has changed so much. When I look at the work we collected in the magazine that was printed at the end of the first year, I find much of it as energetic, moving, funny, gifted as the work we saw in New York.

HOW THE OCEANS FORMED
by Neil Hayward

It all began when God told Noah it would rain for a hundred years. So Noah started to build himself an ark. He just finished putting in the last nail when all the animals, not just half the animals, all the animals came rushing up the ramp because it started sprinkling. All of a sudden it started pouring out and the ark took off. Inside some of the animals were playing tag. Noah said, "We're running out of Budweiser." The animals said, "Who cares?" They were playing hide-and-go-seek. The elephants were playing rock-the-boat. And, of course, the boat was rocking. Then, suddenly, Noah said, "Look!" And they saw four ditches. The boat was rocking so much that all the water went in the ditches. And the boat stopped in sand. And the boat stopped rocking. They stopped right where they started. So that's how the oceans were formed.

I WISH
by Shelly Hayward and Cindy Gardner

I wish I was
*   a black and white*
*   polkadotted cat,*
But really I am a girl
*   with short hair*
*   who used to have long hair.*

I wish I was Leo the Lion,
*   but really I am a girl*
*   with a cat at home.*
I wish I was a bride
*   and I'm getting married on November 31st*
But really I am seven
*   so I can't get married.*

MY DREAM ABOUT THE BEAVER

by Adina Hoffman

I was walking through the woods
*   up the hill*
*   to the beaver dam.*
I went down to the water and a beaver
*   came to me and crawled*
*   up to my knee*
and we went home together.
I got on my pajamas and went to bed
I put the beaver in a fish tank
*   where he could sleep.*
In the morning I got on my bathing suit
and I went to the beaver dam.
And I went down the hill and I dumped the beaver
*   out of the fish tank*
*   and we swam to the shore.*
And we went on to the dry place
*   and lay out in the sun*
*   and then I felt I wanted to go back.*
So I went to the store and I bought the beaver
*   a big large tank.*
And the beaver lived in it.

What happened? I think we can take some credit for hitting on approaches and ideas that excited and engaged the kids and for giving them the sense that writing could be as much a pleasure under some circumstances as it was a pain under others. But we also have to take the blame for some of the early drab work on the basis of which we were too quick to judge the kids. Our hearts weren't in the early efforts, and we brought to them little of the energy and enthusiasm the students needed to get them going.

The disappointment with the early writing was so keen that we began thinking of ways to put aside the writing for all but those who had a special interest in it. For the others the Resource Center would offer a wide variety of other choices—weaving, tie-dyeing, electronics—the whole panoply, which we, as good dilettantes, were eager to learn about as well. In the meantime we carried on with our writing and slowly, miraculously, our initial disappointment gave way to a sense of pleasure and respect.

I think the turning point came when we hit on the idea of a sustained writing project involving older kids in the writing of children's books for the kindergarten. We pulled several children's books off the kindergarten shelves, including Maurice Sendak's *Where the Wild Things Are,* and carried them along to our writing groups, where we read them together and talked about how they were·structured—the way in which the visual and verbal complemented each other; how you could tell a story with a minimum of words, provided they were well-chosen, as in a poem. (Incidentally, although they would be reluctant to admit it, even the fifth and sixth graders could barely conceal their delight at having these wonderful books read to them. What a shame that we insist that kids grow out of certain material, without even the opportunity to go back and be little and wide-eyed once in a while.)

Writing the children's books, making illustrations and the covers, and reading the finished works to the kindergarten kids occupied the better part of the next five weeks in the Resource Center, and for some of the authors it was their finest writing achievement. (NOTE: Examples of this work are difficult to reproduce since so much of their appeal lay in the color illustrations.)

Although there were still many writing days after that which were a dull chore for us and the kids, things were never again quite as frustrating. We were on an upward spiral—generating new ideas, getting better writing from the kids, watching their enjoyment in the process of writing, no longer expecting little of quality from them, becoming enthusiastic about their creations, etc. A particularly pleasing spate of plays came into being in a natural, organic way. The presence of the stage and the roll of brown butcher paper that served as the backdrop for scenery painting was sufficient to set the process in motion. Although we spent a number of weeks doing improvisational one- and two-person exercises on the stage, the actual playwriting did not require any special gimmickry or pump-priming. One or two of the kids would simply make it known that they had an idea for a play. We would help them get it on paper, either in the form of an action outline or as a complete script with dialogue. Then there'd be a round of rehearsals and scene painting, and if it seemed together enough and if the kids wanted it badly enough, a full-fledged performance. Each play inspired others, so that the stage was rarely idle for more than a few weeks.

A good part of the playwriting and rehearsing went on in the course of the two afternoons when the Resource Center was open after school, and it epitomized the kind of open-ended work that usually made those afternoons such a delight.

The other sustained project, which spanned the last five weeks of school, grew out of work that Dick had begun in New York on utopias and imaginary worlds. Tapping what seems to be a universal dislike for geography and social studies texts, we suggested to several of our writing groups that we write our own book about an imaginary country. We settled on a name for the country, either a nonsense word or a word the kids had never seen before that had been culled from the dictionary. The most ominous and ironic name to emerge was the Land of Totalitarian (which didn't turn out to be that kind of place at all). We took the usual geography book section headings—history, industry, mountains, rivers and lakes, religion, etc.—and divided them up and went to work. In the groups where this technique worked best there was a lovely interaction among the kids as they compared notes on their respective sections to make sure that the parts would be consistent with one another—that the animals could inhabit the terrain, that the people had houses that were consonant with whatever quirky traits they had been ascribed, etc. After the appropriate maps and illustrations were added, we typed it all up and had the kids make copies on the ditto machine. We ran out of gas before we could bind the books, but the end product was nonetheless gratifying. It took a whole year to work up to this most ambitious of all our projects, but when we were done we knew we had been somewhere.

That year in the Resource Center was both frustrating and necessary to what followed. We were still at the mercy of the "regular" teachers in the school, who were the keepers of their children's schedules, and in spite of some forays into science, crafts, and local history, we were not considered central to what school was really about. But at the same time we had come to know the children of the town. We were trusted by most of them. It was the ultimate crash course—spending some time each week with every single child in the school from kindergarten to eighth grade, finding out what they were good at and what they were interested in, learning to match up brothers and sisters, cousins and cousins. Perhaps most important of all was what grew out of the after-school sessions. We were making it clear to the kids that our commitment to them did not end at three o'clock, and we were also establishing the fact that the projects that most impressed the kids—the plays, for example— required long blocks of after-school time. After-hours duties may be contrary to union regulations, but even in the best, most energetic classrooms there isn't the time and the concentration during school hours to make big things happen. Many teachers decide that they'd rather live their lives elsewhere, which is fine, provided they recognize that what they can accomplish remains much more limited as a result.

Chapter 3

TEACHERS

The summer after our first year Hazel Flanders, the fifth-sixth grade teacher, announced her retirement, and Dick Murphy and I proposed to the superintendent and the principal that we be hired as a team to replace her and be permitted to split the salary between us. It wasn't a very sound financial proposition, but it was the opportunity we were looking for to put us in more complete control (why is this word an embarrassment?) of a group of children. This particular group was attractive to us because it included the students we had been most deeply involved with in the Resource Center.

To their credit the administrators were receptive to the idea, but they were a little fearful of the community's reaction; so they took the most unusual step of calling an "informational" meeting for the parents of our prospective students to solicit their opinions on our hiring, a decision-making right that the administrators had always fiercely guarded as a professional prerogative. The superintendent surprised us with an eloquent speech on the philosophy of open education, replete with quotes from Piaget on the nature of children's learning. We each spoke briefly about how we would approach our classroom responsibilities, trying to stress popularity-winning points, such as order, self-discipline, reading skills, etc. without misrepresenting what we dreamed of doing in the classroom on our own.

Then came the question and answer period, from which I remember two notable moments. The first was when Reggie Davis got up to speak. Reggie was a native New Yorker who had arrived fifteen or twenty years before us, prospered as an electrician and appliance dealer, and firmly closed the gate behind him in the hope of barring any more outsiders and their ideas. (He had been the most conservative voice on the school board, and a year after this night's information meeting he was stricken with a heart attack and died, after the annual town meeting which had approved by one vote the establishment of a publicly funded kindergarten in Fairlee.)

24

Reggie wondered what someone with a Ph.D. and my list of credentials was doing in a place like Fairlee Elementary School. Something was fishy. Was I, he wondered, running away from a murder rap? The question of my motivation was not one that I had been notably successful in answering for my parents nor many of my friends either. I quickly went through the same account of my past that I've outlined here, talked about my primary concern with happiness in my work. Reggie threw me a quizzical, incredulous look. Just as I had discovered in Mississippi, when folks could discern a motive of self-interest (money, power), they felt reassured, on familiar ground. And failing to detect such a motive did not mean it was absent; it just remained to be uncovered.

The second memorable moment of the meeting came when a work-shirted gentleman I never got to know took the floor to reminisce about what a bore school had been for him, how many inattentive days he had spent at his desk, and how his fondest memories were of a long-gone Fairlee teacher who had square dancing as a regular afternoon activity for her class. His confession and the grunts of recognition it received appeared to be sufficient evidence for the superintendent that our hiring would not result in a midnight firebombing of the school. We were in.

The rest of the summer was a frantic round of planning, building (a workbench, dividers, a science table, shelves), scrounging materials (our predecessor had ordered a box of special penmanship pens and a plastic model of the solar system and had turned back the balance of her supply budget), and frantic reading in areas we had never approached systematically with a group of children—math, social studies, children's literature, sciences. We knew how central the writing was going to be to our program, but we had to decide how much energy we had for planning our own curriculum in each subject area. Our major sacrifice was math, where our materials and approach remained traditional and derivative. It was no worse than what they had been getting, but definitely no better either.

We had thirty-four children and an abundance of space, which included all of the Resource Center and an adjoining classroom that had housed the seventh-eighth grade the previous year. As it turned out, we learned a good deal about the problems of spatial affluence, the difficulties of keeping so much space in good physical shape, and the complexity of supervising and overseeing the work of kids dispersed over such a vast terrain.

The first days of that fall were unending. Managing and being responsible for the movement of so many children for such a long, unbroken time period left us as bone-weary as a steel hauler whose body hasn't yet inured itself to the ceaseless daily pounding. I remember retreating to a little lake front beach after the first day of school, which was also, by the grace of the gods, the hottest day of the summer. Dick and I were thoroughly demoralized and stared off across the water wondering if we hadn't made a terrible mistake. There was a lot about what education professionals call "classroom management" that we were going to have to learn by our lonely selves.

There were a number of memorable projects that evolved over the year. Some of them were the fruits of others' ingenuity, namely the Educational Development Center (EDC) and the Elementary Science Study (ESS), who gave us an entree into the extended study of Eskimos, electricity, pond water, pendulums, the microscope, and mealworms. These curriculum development projects deserve a million thank yous from teachers like us who need some help in defining and entering into certain areas of study without losing our sense of ourselves as curious, creative people who resent being addressed as automatons.

Many projects were of our own invention: an anthropological project called "Growing Up and Growing Old," in which we studied child rearing and aging in different cultures; a local history project, which involved a long look at old town reports, property records, statistics on birth, death, and marriage and interviews with local people about their memories of the Depression, of early auctioneering, and of railroading in the town; and an apprenticeship project, in which students went off to spend full workdays with the local veterinarian, a beauty shop owner, an auto mechanic, etc.

We had also made the disconcerting discovery during our year in the Resource Center that the kids were completely without experience in talking "about" anything of substance among themselves or with adults. During their school time they were talked *at,* required to respond *to* questions, or were just plain buried in their workbooks.

Even rather reticent children have lots of interests they would like to talk about—animals, bikes, horses, television, politics, parents. We decided to include a "discussion" period as a regular part of the weekly schedule. (At various times during the year it occupied anywhere from an hour a week to two hours a day.) The format also varied as the dynamics of the class and the particular subject matter required. But whether we were reading out loud or listening to music, or sounding off or being intimate, this was my favorite time of the day. It was a place to which we could bring some of the things that interested and moved us as adults and that could prove exciting for kids as well—books by Hemingway, Flannery O'Connor, Tolstoy, Malcolm X, Ring Lardner, Elie Wiesel, and the ethologist Farley Mowat; material about slavery, about the history of the American Indian, about World War II, about the concentration camps, about Stravinsky and modern music.

There were lots of days when the kids refused to shut up or quit goosing each other or stop shooting rubber bands, and we came near tears as something that fascinated us never got so much as a nod of acknowledgment from the kids. But there were magical moments when the kids insisted that we go on and on, beyond the time schedule, when my shameless tears were for the finale of a book that had moved me deeply. It was during discussion time that I was at my most messianic, carried along by a sense that I was exposing the children to aspects of the world that they might never otherwise know and that *could* fundamentally affect the way they saw themselves and the world. I've been in a lot of middle-class, suburban-type schools where I felt myself superfluous on a certain level, aware that I brought nothing new to the children, nothing that they wouldn't stumble across in any case at home or from next year's teacher. In Fairlee I felt, somehow, more indispensable.

I also learned some very important lessons about the nature and limits of activity-centered education. So much of what we did in our classroom was concrete and active in the best Piagetian ways—crafts projects, filmmaking, plays, science experiments, measuring activities. What gets lost in the frantic search for the active analogue to everything of importance in the world is the fact that there are matters of the deepest significance that are approachable only through books and words. I find that I must come on like a hoary conservative to make a point that is really a matter of common sense, but somehow innovative education has chosen to become identified with a certain McLuhanish, antiprint position. It began to strike me that a classroom that was emphasizing writing had to pay the proper respect to books and words, had to reflect the centrality of these verbal forms in our own lives.

In order to accommodate these numerous projects and to juggle the range of choices for each student, we had to solve the problem of scheduling. It seems clear to me that the classic distinctions between creativity and order really don't make much sense. You have to be a hell of a good administrator to build a system where children have a modicum of choice and freedom without driving you, their classmates, and themselves absolutely crazy.

After a lot of false starts and abandoned experiments we settled into an arrangement by mid-year that pleased us enough to become a permanent fixture. Each day was divided into five time blocks. Every weekend the kids took a schedule blank home and filled in how they were going to use their time blocks for the week. We would inform them beforehand of any requirements they had to comply with (e.g., everyone must schedule four math periods and two writing periods and two reading periods this week; or no one can schedule time to work on the crafts fair unless they've completed their science notebook). They would also be told to block in time for a film we would see together or a field trip or any other block that group scheduling would not allow them the freedom to alter. These schedules, which had to include details about what you hoped to accomplish each day—how many pages of the book you were reading would you expect to get through, when do you think your story will be finished—had to be approved by a teacher on Monday morning before you got to work. He would also look through your schedule from the previous week to see how close you had come to achieving last week's work commitments and whether, in light of that, you had laid out a realistic amount of work for this week. The kids then filed their schedules in a compartment of one of those shoe bags intended for hanging inside the door of a closet. There it could be easily accessible: to them, if they weren't clear about what they were supposed to be up to; and to us, if we sensed that someone was at loose ends. No bells rang at the ends of periods. If good things were happening, we just ignored the clock and tried to even the score later on. Some days we chucked the schedule entirely and did something special—made scenery for a play, worked on a movie, prepared for a crafts fair. It's fine to be loose and flexible in this way but not so frequently that the kids no longer find the routine schedule credible.

There are many hidden messages in a scheduling process of this kind. Kids can be trusted but also can be called to account on their commitments. Kids can set reasonable goals for themselves. Everyone doesn't have to do the same thing at the same time. And, most interesting for the present purpose, the week's requirements for each subject tell the student something about relative priorities. If you are expected to block out roughly the same number of periods each week for math, reading, writing, science, and linoleum printing you know a lot about what is considered important. (*Note:* I should say here that this subject scheduling arrangement falls short of my ideal of an "integrated day" kind of program in which the focus is on projects, each of which draws on a whole array of skills in a more organic way. In this integrated approach writing as a separate "subject" dissolves into the writing activities that are a necessary and natural part of the write-up of science projects, information-gathering, letters, etc. I'm not a skilled enough teacher yet to manage an operation of that kind, and the abandoning of recognizable "subjects" would have brought me no end of grief from parents.) To have writing, for example, defined as a subject on a par with math and reading tells the student what the teacher takes seriously and, by implication, what the student is expected to follow suit on.

It came as no surprise to the kids in our class that writing was going to play a major role in our classroom. I would guess that they and some of their parents were more surprised to find that we planned to do things besides writing. We had to be careful not to ask for more than two or three writing periods per week so that everyone knew we were serious about the other work areas. The previous year's investment in writing had yielded so many concrete accomplishments—a printed magazine, a produced play, a pile of children's books that had been read appreciatively by the kindergarten kids—that it seemed absurdly effortless to get into writing in our own classroom. Somehow in that year—a long melange of successful and abortive writing gimmicks, buttressed by the attractions of a darkroom, a printing press, and a battery of typewriters—we had managed to convince the kids that the writing was fun and that it had the potential for bringing some recognition from other kids, from parents, and from teachers.

During that first year we had established the practice of taking a group of kids with us whenever we were invited to do a workshop or a presentation for teachers on approaches to writing. There was such a narcissistic charge from reading their work to a group of teachers or doing a writing activity alongside them and being lavishly praised for their prodigal talents. It is akin to the psychic charge that writers get from doing readings, which enable them to return to their work refreshed, assured that there are people out there prepared to love you for your lonely efforts.

The year of groundwork had been absolutely essential. There was no longer any pump-priming necessary. Why are we given to such impatience that we are surprised to discover that children need time to trust themselves and us enough to do the kind of work that springs from deep within, from places that have rarely been acknowledged, let alone encouraged, during "school hours?" Here, for example, is a journal that was literally a gift of trust from Mona, who tells you enough about herself to need no narrator. I'll only say that she spent the first year and a good bit of the second insulting us, both literally and figuratively thumbing her nose at us, trying to work up the courage to be vulnerable.

MY REAL LIFE TIME
by Mona

For about eight years I lived in Bradford on a farm and it was not good at any time any night or day. We had about eight horses, nine dogs, one cat, two bulls, three pigs, and seven baby pigs. Well, it was sort of funn. Sometimes it was sickening. But I wish I could have run away from home.

This is what I had to do: set table, get meals sometimes. I had to get up in the morning at six thirty to help my sisters and brothers do the chores, then in the house again at seven, in time to go to the ugly school house in the morning.

I was in the first grade for two years. I stayed back for one year in first grade. When I was nine I moved to Fairlee away from my family. Because they didn't have enough money to buy our things we needed for home and school. But the first day I moved I was crying because I was taken away from my mother and father. They are living in Fairlee now. I guess it was better today than before. I miss all my old school friends now. I meet some new friends in my school I go to. They come to see me about once a month sometimes. But I have got over that now I hope. I guess. But my life is sad.

I am real good now. I have got a boy I like and he likes me. I guess we are too small to be liking each other, but how can we help it. Now I am still living on another farm again. I miss everything that I knew. But now I have a family that cares about me. It's a real nice family, too. They have a hired hand too. He works in the barn and other things too. He does the milking and feeding the cows sometimes. These are all the animals we have:

These are all the animals we have:	Next, the people
1. 28 cows	1. two mothers
2. 5 baby calves	2. two fathers
3. 49 hens	3. five sisters
4. 11 heifers	4. nine brothers
5. 2 dogs	5. two grand-mothers
6. 9 cats	6. two grand-fathers
7. 1 rooster	7. one niece
8. 2 ducks	8. one hired man
9. 1 lamb	9. one sister-in-law
10. 1 horse	10. nine uncles
11. 1 hamster	11. nine aunts
12. that's all	12. a lot of friends
	13. a lot of cousins

But now on this farm I live on, it is such fun and work. I like living on this farm. We have a pond out back of our barn where we keep our horses. It is fun to swim in the summer and it won't be long before summer's here. I can wear my shorts and other things, too. But now my life is sort of mixed up because when I'm with my mother Clark I want to come home right away. But when I'm here, I never want to see my mother again. But I used to get sick when I went down there. But I guess I'm getting over it now. I still miss my mom and dad Clark. This is what happens when I'm down there:

First thing, I go for a ride.
Second, I watch TV.
Third thing, I play cards or listen to records or we talk to each other about how school is.

Sometimes I most usually watch her knit. I play with my brother Eric and Amy, my niece. Some day I will find out who my brother married. I hope she is good looking and has long hair. But now on to me again. I would take care of myself and be good for my mommy and daddy Clark. But how can I live this way. I can't stand it any longer any more. I was born in Cottage Hospital, January 27, 1961. I am twelve years old now. I am four feet eleven inches tall. I am still growing tall now.

I guess I should tell you about me growing up. I would like a small house to live in. I would like two girls and two boys. The girls names would be April and May. The boys names would be little Freddy and Rocky. This life as me getting married is just a dream. But I wish it would come true. Sometimes I guess nobody would care about me. But now I wish I could live with my real mommy and daddy Clark. I have a lot of friends now, I wish I had my own room now. This summer I hope to baby sit or sell drinks.

My favorite TV show is "Leople, People". This is why I like it. The show is funny sometimes and it is about this doctor and his daughter. When the kids get hurt they go in and see the doctor and he fixes their hurts. What I like about this family—it is a nice family.

In the Waldorf schools, founded on the philosophy of Rudolph Steiner, children are often followed by their teachers through a cycle of four years. Contrast that to the insane practice in some schools of subjecting younger and younger children to departmentalized instruction, as if content took precedence over relationship. Although I recognize the dangers of a child getting stuck in an unsatisfactory relationship with one teacher for several years, I feel that the present system is one that is a model of inefficiency. Just at the point when a teacher is likely to have developed a sufficiently clear sense of a child to be able to design an individualized program, that child is pushed along on the conveyor belt to the next station. We were lucky to have been able to capitalize on two years with our kids.

Let me illustrate by telling you about several of our students: one who left us after a year, one who during his second year took advantage of a wonderful start, and one who emerged from hiding only during that second year.

Chapter 4

THE KIDS

TERRY

In my diaries I find the following, written in late October:

Terry—by far our greatest source of pride so far. A big, hulking, seemingly slow country boy, the last of four sons. His parents are quite old, his father a shrunken little man racked with emphysema. Terry took to us immediately because we were "doing" something. "I could read a book all day and not learn nothing, but when you give me something to do I can learn real fast," says Terry. Kids like Terry are supposed to go to vocational schools where you learn how to do things. (Ever wonder why that privilege is afforded only to "dumb" kids?) But Terry is sharper than anyone imagines. He is an exceptional observer of nature. This week he told me two wonderful stories. First his rabbit was to have babies, one of which would come to the kindergarten. But Terry went out to check the cage one morning and found the mother no longer pregnant, but no babies to be seen. His father told him the buck rabbit killed them, kicked them to death with his hindpaws.

Second, he was down watching the beavers. He saw a beaver slap the water with his tail, which was grabbed by a snapping turtle who would not let go until five beavers ganged up on him. Terry's stories are often about beavers and turtles. He must spend hours alone in the woods.

It was the darkroom that really got him. One day after school he showed up with some old negatives he had found at home. They turned out to be pictures of his grandfather on his farm in Lancaster, New Hampshire, working the field with his team of oxen. The negatives were so old we had no idea what would come out, but the contact prints looked good so I took Terry through the enlargement process. When he saw that blowup take shape in the developer tray, you could almost see his face light up in the dark. We made one copy for him to take home, one to hang on the wall outside the darkroom. His parents decided to frame the one he brought home. Then we asked Terry if he wouldn't like to write up instructions that could guide the other kids in using the enlarger. Terry struggled with it for three days after school, dictating parts of it to Dick, who finally put it on ditto stencils. Terry took home copies of those instructions with the same pride with which he took home the photo. I think it was the first "real" thing he's written.

It's a little success story that we've told many times in many places. Sometimes we neglect to mention that the story has a new ending because somewhere along the way we lost Terry, and I'm not sure anyone's going to find him again. He sat around the Resource Center for a good many weeks, just watching silently; he could sit that way for hours without allowing a single cue to his inner musing cross his face. Several times he mentioned that he had an idea for a play, although he was sure no one would want to act in it. We said we'd like to help him write it, but we never got around to it. There were so many other kids swarming around the Resource Center by then that we always managed to overlook his silent presence. He and Dick talked about going off snowshoeing in the woods, but that never happened either. After a while he stopped hanging around after school but spent many idle hours during the day horsing around with his seventh and eighth grade classmates when there were no workshop groups scheduled. We discovered how destructive Terry could be. In his quiet, sullen way he left behind a trail of broken equipment, spilled chemicals, torn paper; until one day in a moment of anger over one or another of these assaults, we asked him to stay out of the Resource Center for a week.

You could feel the anger rolling off Terry in waves, and the angrier he got the guiltier we felt. We kept saying that we *had* to do something with/about/for Terry, but our sporadic efforts were just too strained to repair the broken ties. From time to time he would relax enough to tell us about some excursion into the woods or about a dead fawn he had seen on the highway, and at those times his face would light up and his speech would show some of the surprisingly complex verbal wit that few people dreamed he was capable of, but that was rare.

HOW TO ENLARGE YOUR PRINT
by Terry Hoyt

1. *First you make sure there's no light that can get in the darkroom.*
2. *Then you turn on the safety light, and plug in the enlarger.*
3. *Take the negative carrier out of the developer. The negative carrier is a semi-circle piece of metal in the middle of the developer. Pull it out and open it up.*

34

This is what the negative carrier looks like:

This is where to find it in the enlarger.

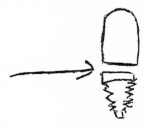

4. *Put the negative, dull side down, into the negative carrier. Make sure the negative is straight.*
5. *Now put the negative carrier back into the enlarger.*
6. *Put some clean, white typing paper on the easel at the bottom of the enlarger. This paper will show you how your finished enlargement will look. This is what the easel looks like:*

7. *There are two red knobs which you can adjust to make a larger or smaller enlargement. The knob in back lets you slide the whole enlarger up and down the pole. (UP always makes the print larger, DOWN makes it smaller.) Now use the larger red knob to focus.*

35

Look carefully at the paper, until you can see everything in your picture very clearly.

8. *You can get a lighter or darker print by turning the black knob at the bottom of the lense.*

   Here are all the knobs for adjusting height, focus, and light:

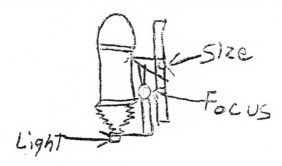

9. *Now you are ready to print. Turn off the enlarger light. Take a piece of enlargement paper, and cut a two inch strip. Draw lines every two inches along the strip. Find a piece of cardboard to slide along the strip. You need to watch a clock with a second hand or have a stopwatch. Use the strip to help you decide which is the best exposure.*

10. *Put the strip on the easel. Turn on the light. Slide the cardboard along the strip stopping at the lines you've marked. Expose the first section of the strip 10 seconds, the second 10 seconds, the third another 10, and so on, up to one minute.*

11. *Put the test strip into the first bath for about one minute. (You may want to take the test strip out earlier if it starts to get too dark.)*

    Here is how the test strip should look:

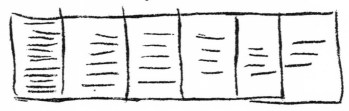

12. *Put the test strip into the second bath, the stop bath, for fifteen seconds.*

13. *Now put it in the third bath, the fixer, for five to ten minutes.*

14. *Now put the strip into the sink and let cold water run over it.*

15. *Look at the strip, find the best exposure. This will tell you how long to expose the enlargement.*
16. *Turn out the enlarger light again. Take a full sheet of enlargement paper. Place it on the easel. Everything should be focussed and ready to go. Turn on the light and print. Develop in the three baths just as before, then run the enlargement under cold water.*
17. *Dry the enlargement in the electric dryer and press flat between the plywood frame.*

Dick, Sheila, and Posey went to the graduation in the Town Hall and watched Terry, his two hundred-odd pounds straitjacketed in an unfamiliar suit, go through the pathetic ceremony with his thirteen classmates. It filled them with sadness, they said, to realize that this sad little graduation would probably be the first and the last in Terry's life.

I've seen him from time to time since school is over. Often when I drive up on the highway, I can see him up on a tractor across the frontage road, cutting hay for the farmer on whose land Terry's family lives. The other day I saw him in the hardware store standing alongside his boss in his work clothes. He looked tanned from outdoor work, and his hair was blonder than I remembered. I was pleased to see him. "What you been doing, Terry?" Terry half-turned his head away, as if to blot out the sight of me. "Nothin'."

JOHN

Where was he at the beginning of the year? It's amazing how long it takes for some kids to enter your field of vision. Not that John is the shy, retiring type. I just wasn't ready to see him. Perhaps I was still looking for the archetypal country boys, freckled and blond-haired. John couldn't be further from that. He's an eleven-year-old version of the vintage Beatle-look—long, dark hair, almost bowl-cut, framing his round, shining face.

I had a brief moment of awareness of what was in store with John during one of our early writing groups. We were discussing dreams in preparation for asking the kids to put some of theirs on paper. John began to describe what turned out to be a perfect deja vu experience—going to hang up his coat, he stopped dead in his tracks, convinced that he had played out precisely that same scene before. It takes an extraordinary self-awareness to be attuned to that kind of experience and an equally extraordinary combination of openness and verbal facility to share it unself-consciously with others. I made a mental note of all that and filed it away.

John was in one of our fifth-sixth grade writing groups that we called our "All-Stars," half-jokingly, as if to conceal the fact that they *were* our favorite group of kids. We took great delight in the discussions with them at the beginning of each session, in which the kids outdid each other in their hilarious accounts of some movie they had seen on TV with an impossibly labyrinthine plot or of the most recent misdeeds of their classroom teacher. John took the lead in these verbal fireworks and proved himself a master of the kind of preadolescent pop culture that I remember revering as a form of high art at that age. John was fun to listen to and fun to talk with.

John's kind of gifts were not too highly honored by his regular teacher, who tended to see him as impudent and a bit irresponsible. Since he is basically a polite and respectful boy (though he wasn't above complaining after the fact), he did not waste energy in rebellion against her (I don't think I've seen any of that New York-style rebelliousness from anyone here); instead he stored it all away and put it to good use in the Resource Center. It was kids like John who made us feel that the presence of the Resource Center was justified if only to serve them. For him it was an alternative to a formal, rigid classroom, in which his sense of perspective allowed him to survive, but which left him very little room to grow.

It was a constant source of amazement that kids like John could spring up, like wildflowers, in a place like Fairlee. Something had to be going on in his family, which, though not unusual in any flamboyant way, took obvious pride and pleasure in the intelligence and sensitivity of John and his two older brothers. John's mother, an extremely intelligent and lively woman whose attractive face is almost concealed by her graying hair and her excess weight, once took us into the boys' room at home to show us the outrageous patchwork of colors they had painted it. She said it was outrageous, but her eyes said she loved it. She also showed us her husband's cactus collection, which overflowed all the downstairs rooms, a carryover from the days when he ran a greenhouse in northern Maine before he moved here to manage a local college's supply room.

John in the darkroom or John working on his play was always the picture of purposefulness. He knew that we took pride in his work, and we knew that he enjoyed being with us, and somehow the combination spurred him on to more and more impressive efforts. Although he was not the kind of kid who was motivated by the need for praise or reward, the appreciation he got from us and from the other kids brought on a kind of heady feeling that carried him along. John onstage playing the leading role in his Clifford Irving play delivered inspired ad lib lines. He was a ham prolonging the delicious moments in the limelight, and he could tell from the laughs that his audience was just as eager to prolong them.

On the car rides to and from the teacher workshops, John could be the silly, giddy, coltish eleven year old that he had every right to be. Giggling over the universal dirty jokes, punching, pinching, wrestling, shouting worn camp songs—John knew how to play with all his being, and this was the great gift he brought to his more "serious" work.

Here, for posterity, is John's Clifford Irving memorial!

THE GREAT HOAX
(A play in five scenes)
by John Durgin

Cast of Characters

Clifford Irving	*— the writer*
Edith Irving	*— his wife*
Richard the Rip	*— President of Nixon, Inc., largest publishing company in the world*
Christopher Columbus	*— who is never seen on stage but is heard*

The bank teller
Narrator

SCENE I

Place: The Irvings' apartment
Characters: Clifford and Edith Irving

Narrator:　　　　　*We now take you to the apartment of Clifford Irving and Edith Irving in Harlem.*

(Clifford and Edith are sitting at a table with a coffin on top of it as the curtain comes up.)

Edith:　　　　　*Clifford, all you ever do around this apartment is sit at the table writing a biography of Howard Hughes. It hasn't brought us any money yet. You haven't sold a single copy. I want to go to Switzerland. I want a fur coat and a Honda. I want to move to a new apartment. I want some new furniture and some new carpeting. Why don't you go out and make some money?*

39

Clifford:	*You'll have all that when I'm through with my master plan.*
Edith:	*I've heard about your master plans before, and we still never have any money. I want a trip to Switzerland. I want you to do something! And when are you going to get this dirty coffin out of my living room?*
Clifford:	*But the coffin is part of my master plan. You see, we will write a fake interview with Christopher Columbus, and then we will take it to the publishing company, Nixon, Inc. We will say that we will sell the interview to them for $650,000. (After all, interviews with dead people are hard to come by.) We'll say that we've invented a serum that makes dead people answer any questions that are asked. That's why I brought the coffin home. We'll say that we dug it up from Christopher Columbus' grave in Arlington Cemetery.*
Edith:	*Hmmm, Clifford, that sounds like the first good idea you've had since we've been married.*
Clifford:	*Here, you take this biography of Howard Hughes and put it away in a drawer, and get the typewriter and a couple of pieces of paper, and we'll get to work.*

(Edith stands up and gets the paper and typewriter.)

Clifford:	*Now, I'll dictate, you type.* *"Question: Where were you born?* *Answer: Genoa, Italy.* *Question: When did you die?* *Answer: 1506."*

(The typewriter begins clicking away as the curtain slowly comes down.)

SCENE II

Place: The top of the Empire State Building.
Characters: Clifford and Edith Irving, and Richard the Rip

(Enter Clifford and Edith. Clifford carries a muddy shovel.)

Edith:	How come we had to walk up all the stairs to the top of the Empire State Building? Why did we have to meet here? Why couldn't we meet in our apartment? Clifford, you know I never liked high places. You know I'm nervous about this plan, anyway. It'll probably never turn out anyhow, and we'll be sued by the company.
Clifford:	Edith, will you stop complaining. Leave it to me. This is all part of my master plan. If you would only listen to me, instead of babbling away all the time. Shhh, here comes someone now......

(Enter Richard the Rip)

Richard the Rip:	*(very proudly)* Hello, hello, hello, hello. *(He shakes everyone's hand)* I'm Richard the Rip, President, Chief of Staff, Treasurer, and Chairman of the Board of Nixon, Incorporated, we're the biggest and best publishing company in the world...if you don't mind my saying so. *(whispers)* Actually, we make so much money on our printing, it's pathetic. Now, what can I do for you about this Christopher Columbus business?
Clifford:	Well, Dick, — you don't mind if we call you Dick, do you? *(with a little nervous laugh)* We have in our hands the one and only interview with Christopher Columbus. We have the secret for getting more interviews from him. How would you like to pay us for our work?
Richard the Rip:	Very interesting, very interesting, very interesting. Yes, let me take a look at that first interview.
Clifford	Okay, Dick, here it is.

*(Clifford and Edith exchange nervous glances back and forth
and Richard the Rip reads)*

41

Richard the Rip:	Well, it certainly sounds like Christopher Columbus. But I want proof. Tell me again now, how did you get this interview?
Edith:	Well, first my darling husband—who's one of the wisest men around—my husband and I went to Arlington Cemetery....

(Clifford gives her a weird look)

Edith:	We dug up Christopher Columbus, and we put his body in the back of our beautiful Model "A" Ford. Look, here's the muddy shovel that we used. Then we drove back to our luxurious apartment in Harlem. When we got there, my brilliant husband injected his body with a special serum.
Clifford:	That's right, Edith. With my special serum I can ask dead people any question, and they must answer. In a few years, I shall know all of history's secrets. I will interview people such as George Washington, Abe Lincoln, etcetera. Dick, if you and I work together, we can be the richest people on earth, even richer than J. Paul Getty.
Richard the Rip:	What you are saying is very interesting. But I still must have proof. Even though I'm very rich, I don't throw my money away. I demand to come to your apartment, or no deal.
Clifford & Edith:	Okay, we'll meet tomorrow night at midnight at our apartment. And then you'll be able to talk to Christopher Columbus yourself.
Richard the Rip:	Very well, see you tomorrow. Say, would you like to fly down to the street in my chauffeur-driven, Jumbo 747?
Edith:	Sure, anything's better than climbing up and down these stairs.

(Curtain)

SCENE III

Place: Back at the Irvings' apartment in Harlem.
Characters: Clifford and Edith Irving, and Richard the Rip.

(Edith and Clifford are making last minute preparations for the visit of Richard the Rip. Edith starts dusting off the casket, Clifford is putting the serum in the needle.)

Clifford: Edith, stop dusting off the casket. Are you crazy or something? We want to make it look like it's the dirt from Arlington Cemetery.

Edith: Don't worry about it. I'm just tidying up a bit. And, I'll tell you, this plan of yours had better work, 'cause this is the last time I'm ever going to clean this apartment.

Clifford: Don't worry, it will. We'll be off to Switzerland after this scheme.

(Suddenly, there is a knock on the door)

Clifford: Who's there?

Richard the Rip: It's me, Richard the Rip, President, Chief of Staff, Treasurer, and Chairman of the Board of Nixon, Incorporated, the biggest and best publishing company in the world.

Clifford & Edith: *(together)* Oh, please come in, Dick. Do sit down. Make yourself comfortable, Dick. Oh, take this chair, it's the most comfortable. Make yourself at home, Dick. Would you like a drink, Dick? Scotch and beer?

Richard the Rip: No thank you. I never drink when I'm working. I want to get right to the point. Where is your Christopher Columbus?

(He is sitting right in front of the coffin)

Clifford & Edith: Right here in front of you.

Richard the Rip: Oh, sorry, I didn't notice him.

Clifford: I think we're ready to begin...... Edith, the serum!

(Clifford slowly opens the casket, an arm flops out. Clifford injects his magic serum into the arm, then he throws the arm back into the coffin)

43

Clifford:	*It will take thirty seconds for this serum to take effect. (He looks at his watch) Then we will be able to ask Christopher Columbus any question, and he must give us a direct answer. Time's up. Dick, you can ask the first question.*
Richard the Rip:	*Christopher Columbus, when did you discover America?*
Columbus:	*1492.*

(Richard the Rip thinks for awhile, then nods slowly)

Richard the Rip:	*What were the names of your ships?*
Columbus:	*The Pinta, Nina and the Santa Maria.*
Richard the Rip:	*Where were you born?*
Columbus:	*Genoa, Italy.*
Richard the Rip:	*By God, Clifford. I think you've really got something. Let me think of some more good questions.*
Clifford:	*Well, you can ask one or two more questions, but the serum is going to wear off soon, and he's likely to give some wrong answers.*
Richard the Rip:	*Where was the first English settlement made?*
Columbus:	*Mount Vernon.*
Clifford:	*Well, it's obvious that the serum is wearing off.*
Richard the Rip:	*Very good, very good, very good. I never thought that I would come across an interview with Christopher Columbus. This is miraculous! Amazing! I am prepared to personally give you a check for $650,000 from the biggest and best publishing company in the world, Nixon, Inc.*

(He writes the check)

Clifford:	*Well, it's been nice seeing you, Dick. You just go right home now, and don't worry about a thing. We'll have the book on Christopher Columbus ready in a week. This is only the beginning of the money we will make together.*
Richard the Rip:	*Thank you, thank you, thank you. We'll make next week's edition of Time-Life. I'll be richer than ever!*

(The Irvings push him out the door. Richard the Rip pokes his head back)

Richard the Rip: Oh, by the way, I will be seeing you next week, won't I?

Clifford & Edith: Sure, sure, sure. Goodbye *(whispering)* sucker!

(The door closes. Clifford and Edith dance around kissing the check)

Edith: At last! My new furniture. My Honda. My fur coat. We can move out of Harlem to our new apartment. Our trip to Switzerland!

Clifford: Let's celebrate.

(He puts on a record, "Just an Old Fashioned Love Song," and pours two huge drinks)

Clifford: Tomorrow we'll charter our 747 to Switzerland, and we'll make reservations at the Ritz.

(They dance around together and drink their drinks)

Edith: *(getting a little drunk now)* Oh, my dearest Clifford. I'm sorry I said that you would never make any money. I apologize. I understand now what a genius you really are. Can you ever forgive me, Clifford?

Clifford: Yes, Edith, all is forgiven. We begin our new life together today.

Edith: Oh, Clifford, I'm so happy. I feel that I want to dance.

(She jumps up on the table and the casket and starts dancing with a lampshade on her head)

Edith: Oh, my Honda, my new fur coat, my......

Clifford: Edith, there's just one problem. You never learned how to hold your liquor.

(The curtain goes down)

SCENE IV

Place: The Irvings' apartment.
Characters: Richard the Rip

    (Enter Richard the Rip, he starts knocking on the door)

Richard the Rip: Hmmmmm. That's funny. I wonder why no one answers.

    (He knocks again a little louder)

    Didn't they say that we would meet here today again? Hello, Hello. Is anybody home? Clifford? Edith?

(Still no answer. He starts to kick the door)

    If no one answers in three seconds I'll bust th s door down. Hello, Hello. It's me. Richard the Rip. President, Chief of Staff, Treasurer, and Chairman of the Board of Nixon, Inc., the biggest and best publishing company in the world. I demand that you open up! They can't do this to me. I'll break down the door.

    (He smashes the door down)

    Well, at least Christopher Columbus is still here. Since no one's around, I think I'll take a look inside.

(He opens the casket on the table, and pulls out a tape recorder.
His mouth falls open in amazement as the curtain falls)

SCENE V

Place: The Swiss National Bank, in Geneva, Switzerland.
Characters: The Bank Teller, Clifford and Edith Irving.

    (Clifford and Edith enter the bank.
    The Bank Teller waits on them)

Clifford & Edith: Hello.

Bank Teller: Good day to you.

(They hand the check to the Bank Teller along with a deposit slip)

Clifford & Edith:	*We'd like to deposit this check, please.*
Bank Teller	*Why certainly.*
Clifford:	*Please deposit the check in the name of Howard Hughes.*

(Final Curtain)

The second year for John in our classroom opened on the high pitch that carried over from the success of the previous year's play. There was no question in John's mind that he would embark on another play. All that remained were the bothersome details of choosing a topic, writing a script, making the costumes and sets, putting it on, and accepting the accolades. But John soon made the humbling discovery—which has been shared by young violin prodigies, authors of brilliant first novels, and great little league pitchers: the second time around isn't so easy.

John's metier was clearly political, his orientation to current events. He searched through the newspapers and was attracted to Nixon, who after all was only a bit player in the first play. Nixon may have been fertile ground for the cartoonists, but Philip Roth demonstrated that literary parody requires larger-than-life characters to begin with. Cardboard caricatures can't be propped up long enough to get knocked down. John abandoned that task.

One could sense that anxiety was building. It wasn't to be so easy after all. One day Dick brought to class one of those magazine pieces that seems to be reprinted in its entirety every three years in certain magazines. This one was about J. Paul Getty, "the richest man in the world." John's house sat almost directly across from the Getty station on the town's main street, a fact that I imagine must have crystallized his interest in the man.

Between that inception and the production of "The Getty Ripoff" at the end of the year laid a minefield of frustration, false starts, and frayed tempers. It took John half the year to complete the script, this in spite of countless after-school writing sessions with Dick, and the rest of the year to see it through to completion. The plot and the dialogue just did not flow. John wisecracked and horseplayed his way through this dry period. He accomplished a lot less in his other schoolwork than he was capable of, worked on only a few other writing projects during the year, and often left Dick regretting the existence of both John and "Mr. Greedy."

Yet what emerged from that process was what I consider to be one of the funniest, most sophisticated "student" plays I have read. For

John there were some important lessons along the way about the creative process and its wily ways. (See appendix)

John had two more years remaining in the Fairlee School after we left each other. They were a nightmare. His teachers mistook his wit and sophistication for disrespect. They gave him nothing to which he could devote himself and his considerable energies. I got a call from John's mother one evening in the second year after we had left. John had been manhandled, tossed around the classroom and the school office by the assistant superintendent, who had been called to the school to investigate complaints of disrespectful behavior by students. John and his classmates swore that he had done nothing wrong but was being scapegoated. Nevertheless John was under instructions from his mother not to talk back, to say "yes, Sir" and "no, Sir," regardless of provocation, and to leave the righting of injustices to her. The assistant superintendent thought the "yes, Sir" routine was tongue-in-cheek (how could he have helped but sense the anger underneath it), and it drove him to fits of even greater rage.

John's mother demanded an apology and an assurance that it wouldn't happen again. The assistant superintendent contended that none of it had ever happened. John learned a two-fold bitter lesson about adult frailty when, first, his teacher refused to speak out in John's behalf, although she had seen the entire incident; and second, when his parents folded in the face of the unyielding administration and demonstrated that they could not in fact protect him from injustice. They chose the survivors' strategy of clenching their fists and sliding through the balance of the year when John would be done with the Fairlee school. It was all such a small injustice to John and such a small act of cowardice by his parents, but in the more innocent and trusting world of rural Vermont, one might guess that it burned as deeply as the grosser indignities of Bedford-Stuyvesant or blue-collar Newark.

John has now moved on to the regional high school, a place of greater sophistication and more ample breathing space. His mother tells me that his teachers seem to like him. Last week John brought the plays to his English teacher who admired them. Perhaps he is to get a reprieve.

MICHAEL (From the first year journals)

North of town on Highway 5 there is a string of neatly kept pink cottages that, according to the sign out front, constitute the Hollywood Motel. They are owned by Michael's parents, a French-Canadian couple who have literally built the place with their own hands and maintain it with no little sweat and worry, I would guess. Our heart sinks when we drive by and see the premises empty except for the ten-year-old Cadillac that belongs to Michael's father. Across the road is a newer brick motel whose rooms face out on a drive-in movie, so that customers get a free look at the evening's feature. Whatever transient business comes by on that highway is more likely to be drawn there than to the Hollywood—minus flicks.

That motel seems so much like Michael himself: the embodiment of virtue that is likely to go unrewarded. I have never seen a "gooder" boy than Michael. With his long lashes, small, frail build, and piping prepubescent voice, he is the perfect choirboy to play alongside Bing Crosby-as-parish-priest in some 1940s movie. I think I can reconstruct from my own "good boy" days what it feels like inside Michael's skin: a pervasive aura of righteous feeling built from all the accumulated praise of parents and teachers who find you the model untroublesome boy, the kind of kid your friends are being urged by their parents to emulate. Michael is such a sweet, compliant boy that he had no trouble winning favor with his very strict teacher this past year. The wonder is that he was not at the same time ostracized by the other kids for his role as something of a teacher's pet. They affectionately call him "Nuts"—a play on his real last name—love him for his gentleness, and seem willingly to overlook the fact that he is a hopelessly weak and uncoordinated athlete.

There are serious long-term drawbacks to being a good boy. As you get older the hard edges of self have little around which to take shape. So much pliability and such a primacy of doing what grown-ups expect of you doesn't leave you with many cues to go on when you're on your own. And, in the present, it doesn't make very promising soil for the kinds of writing we were doing in the Resource Center. It was hard to imagine Michael being loose enough or crazy enough to write a set of outrageous lies or an account of what it would be like to live in a radioactive house. I can't remember anything that Michael wrote during the first eight months of the year.

But there were other things in the Resource Center that did engage Michael deeply and indicate to us that there was lots of good, healthy, self-motivated curiosity behind that compliant exterior. Michael was absolutely fascinated by the printing press and the darkroom. He began coming religiously to the after-school sessions so that he could have a go at them and at the electronics and science materials. On those rare days when he couldn't stay after school, he approached me with the news with a mournful, apologetic look as if he feared that he might be failing or offending me by his impending absence. But I knew that he was also genuinely sorry to be missing out on the fun.

He began borrowing books and pamphlets on science experiments and darkroom techniques from the Resource Center, and within a short time he mastered the photographic processes to the point where he was in constant demand as a consultant on developing rolls of film, making contact prints, etc. I can't say that he ever did anything of great quality in the darkroom, but he was genuinely proud and excited about what he was able to do. After Christmas vacation he returned from a visit to his Canadian relatives with a roll of film of the Chateau Frontenac and other sights around Quebec City. He worked hard on printing and developing these, and he told me his parents were pleased with them when he brought them home. It seemed to me a fine merging of his typical efforts to please with an activity that brought its own reward.

I don't know what the cause-effect relationship is, but in the last big writing project of the year, the imaginary world, Michael achieved something of a breakthrough. He chose to write about religion in the country of Delphin, an altogether unpromising subject for a boy like Michael. But it was perfectly wonderful, funny and imaginative—all the things that Michael seemed incapable of before. I suspect that all this had something to do with the other things that Michael found pleasure in around the Resource Center and the growing sense of what he might be capable of, as well as of what was permissible in our strange room.

Michael's last fling in the Resource Center came in Posey's tie-dyeing sessions. He wanted very much to learn how to do it, and he brought in a bag full of sheets to experiment on. After one particularly successful session in the last weeks of school, Posey drove by the motel and was amazed to see a clothesline full of Michael's multicolored creations flapping in the breeze behind the pink cottages. His parents must have liked them too.

Those beginning breakthroughs of that first year grew and solidified —or do breakthroughs lead to shatterings?—in the second year. Michael actually learned to be naughty and I'm proud to have been a party to that corrupting process. I can see Michael pushing and being pushed on line, trading punches to the biceps, the closest equivalents some preadolescent boys have to signs of affection. Michael teamed up with the "baddest" boy in the class to work on a collaborative writing project—a play about Sir Walter Raleigh that was long and undistinguished but that meant a great deal in the doing to both David and Michael. David was a fine choice for Michael: a worldly, sophisticated boy who had moved to Fairlee from suburban Connecticut after a venomous split between his parents. He was a bright, troubled boy given to bragging, thought by some townsfolk to be engaged in shoplifting, and undoubtedly more knowledgeable about sex than his country cousin classmates. He and Michael stood to learn a lot from each other: one about the confusions and uncertainties of the larger world, the other about the security of a small community and an inseparable family.

Chapter 5

THE WRITING PROGRAM

The structure of the writing program was remarkably undistinguished. Each student scheduled himself/herself for a minimum of two to three writing periods each week. During a writing period you were expected to be in the Resource Center, as opposed to the adjoining classroom, which was reserved for "noisier" activities like science, although, in fact, this distinction was never recognized by the kids and was inconsistently enforced by us. During any work period either Dick or I was stationed in the Resource Center, often with a student teacher as well, and we served as combination consultant, oracle, secretary, arbiter, or sergeant-at-arms. Each student would go off with his/her writing folder to a table, a rug space, a hidden corner, a perch atop or beneath our two-tiered typing platform, the asphyxiating but quiet atmosphere of the darkroom, or a leaning space against the outside wall of the school on sunny days. Since the folders remained in the Center, we had an opportunity every few days to look over the students' work and see how they were progressing.

It was necessary to do this because there were long periods when certain students were entirely on their own. They had set a task for themselves that didn't require our day-to-day involvement. This was exactly what we had dreamed of during those dreary days the previous year when the kids would wander into the Resource Center wearing their vacant "what-are-we-supposed-to-do?" stares. Two earnest, but essentially uninspired, students took to writing novellas of 90-100 pages, which they loved to read aloud, to our dismay. These were both children from whom we could barely extract a page of writing the previous year. There were numerous other projects of many weeks' duration that required minimal adult attention once they were underway. John's success with his plays assured that at least four or five plays were always in progress; three or four boys were sure to be in the midst of a fifteen-page Walter Mittyish account of a basketball game between Fairlee and some nonexistent patsy or a long account of an auto race in which Dick and I were forever piloting our machines to last place finishes.

I will spare you the reproduction of these epics, which make terrible reading for adult eyes but which are worthy of mention precisely because they underscore the need for a double standard in judging children's writing. Some of it is moving and brilliant; some is remarkably soporific. The authors and their young audiences love it, but not adults. In anthologies of student writing this work is usually censored out, and the unwitting audience of fellow teachers or writers just can't understand why their kids generally write such tiresome stuff and not the timeless morsels of the published anthology.

Here is a more readable sample of unsupervised writing, an insanely spirited parody of the kind of horse stories that girls of a certain age seem capable of consuming by the dozen. This story constitutes a bit of leg-pulling by two boys in the class who detested the horse books. If you could see the original copy I have in front of me, you would discover that none of the chapters are typed or transcribed in the handwriting of one of the teachers, usually a sure sign of a cry for help from student to teacher. (I want to return to the question of parody in children's writing for a more detailed discussion later.)

THE REVOLT OF THE RED, WHITE, AND BLUE STALLION OF FARLEY ISLAND

"Little eight-year old Alec dreamed of owning his own horse as long as he could remember. (About five years.)"

AN ALL AMERICAN HORSE STORY

Published by Murphy and Typewriter, Inc.
Copyright 1972-1973
First Edition
Blake Street
Fairlee, Vermont 05045

NOTICE: No part of this story may be written over without the permission of John Christopher Durgin or Lawrence Clifford Farnham.

CHAPTER I

"Happy Birthday"

It was Tuesday, August sixteenth. Tomorrow was Alec's birthday. Alec's Uncle Ralph was coming to visit him. He was seventy years old and owned a Honda. All Alec could think about was owning a horse.

Alec's mother was in the kitchen making a surprise cake for Alec. Alec yawned and walked into the kitchen. His mother said, "Go out and fill up this quart bottle with milk. Bessy's out in the pasture. She won't mind."

Alec walked out of the door and slammed it behind him. The door fell off its hinges. He mumbled to himself "stupid door." Then he kicked the milk bucket all the way across the field. When he got to Bessy the bucket was full of holes and dents. Alec mumbled, "I wish Uncle Ralph would come."

Alec put the milk bucket under Bessy and started to milk her. He did not know the milk was going straight thru the holes in the bucket into Cline's mouth, his pet cat. Cline is not an ordinary cat. He was run over by Alec's seventy year old Uncle when he was learning how to drive his Honda.

Since then Cline has not been able to meow right. It sounded like a cow, a sick moo. Often he was mistaken for Bessy. Alec finished and noticed that Cline had taken all the milk. He had a swelled stomach. Alec said, "What duh heck," and walked back to the house.

Just as he walked thru what was the screen door he heard a motorcycle engine. To this he yelled, "Uncle Ralph is here!" Alec threw the bucket into the air. The bucket landed on his mother's head who was just coming thru the door. Alec started to race out but suddenly stopped. To his surprise Uncle Ralph had a red, white and blue horse strapped to his sissy bar.

CHAPTER II

"The Revolt of the Red, White, and Blue Stallion"

It was a cloudy day and Uncle Ralph told Alec to put Filly in the pasture for a half an hour before the tropical storm that was predicted set in. Alec rode Filly out to the pasture and dismounted. Alec walked back to the house and went inside.

His mother and father were just starting a game of Crazy Eights. His mother asked him to join in. They were so much involved in the game they didn't notice the thunder and lightning outside. Just as Alec was picking up a four of hearts there was a big crash of lightning. He had some beer and a piece of cake. When Alec jumped up the table flipped over. The cake went into Uncle Ralph's face and the beer went all over his mother's new Oriental dress. Uncle Ralph's Playboy Magazine was completely ruined and the centerfold was shriveled up. Alec yelled, "Filly! She's out in the pasture!"

Immediately everyone ran to the door. They got stuck in the doorway. No one could move. They waited for about sixty seconds. Then Uncle Ralph had an idea. He said, "You two go forward and I'll go backward."

One. Two. Three. Crack! The door frame broke up into a million pieces. They all ran to Filly. There lay Filly on the ground. Alec walked over to Filly and put his hand down to pat her. But the second he touched her he got a shock. His nose lit up. He looked like Rudolf the Second.

Alec walked away. His Uncle said, "You just had a shocking experience, sit down." Alec started to sit down but slipped in some fresh horse manure and landed face first in it.

Uncle Ralph said he told us before that Filly had been a high voltage horse. This is to be remembered as, "The Revolt of Filly."

CHAPTER III

"The Last of Uncle Ralph"

It was Thursday and it was time for Uncle Ralph to leave. He had his bags all packed. He went into the barn to get his Honda. He tried to start it up, but the plug was fouled up with manure from Filly. He took the garden hose, and hosed down the motorcycle. He then sprayed his Honda with Lysol. Uncle Ralph roped on his suitcases to the sissy bar. He kicked the starter with his foot, the engine started but it sounded like manure going through the engine. And that's just what it was. The leftover manure was coming out the tail pipe. Alec came through the door that very moment. Immediately all the manure covered him. Alec stood there covered with manure saying cuss words to his Uncle, "!!???****!..you****???'!''!"bleep bleep bleeeeeeeep person." Uncle Ralph's mouth fell open in surprise. Quickly Alec scraped manure off his face and threw it at Uncle Ralph. Then Alec ran in the barn and hid under the hay. Uncle Ralph went in the house to get cleaned. Alec's mother screamed and asked what happened. Uncle Ralph replied, "Your stupid son, he threw manure in my face!" Alec's mother asked Uncle

Ralph what he did to make Alec throw the manure. Uncle Ralph replied, "Well...Well...Nothing!" Uncle Ralph stomped out. Alec's mother heard the motorcycle. She looked out the window and saw Uncle Ralph pop a wheely while he was going down the lane. This was the last they saw of Uncle Ralph.

CHAPTER IV

"Filly, Alec and the Rubber Saddle"

Filly was thirty-two years old. Alec realized that the time had come to begin her training. He needed a saddle. He wrote to his father who worked with Dupont to get the latest information about saddles. His father wrote that Dupont had just invented a new synthetic rubber saddle.

Alec dreamed about the saddle. He could picture himself riding over to Jack Host's house and showing him his rubber saddle. He knew Jack would be jealous.

Finally the day arrived. The Parcel Post truck brought the package to Alec's house. Alec was all excited. He signed for it and took it to the house. He took a one-edged razor blade and opened it up. He immediately took the saddle out to Filly to try it on. But the moment he tried to put it on he got a shock. So Alec ran back to the house to get some Playtex rubber gloves. He found some gloves under the sink. He put them on and ran out to Filly. He picked up the saddle and put it on Filly. This time he didn't get a shock. Alec hitched the strap and put the bridle on her. Then carefully he put one of his feet on the stirrup; then he got on. Alec said, "All right, Filly, getup."

Filly started into a fast gallop. But after 12 yards, she stopped. Alec almost fell off. Alec said getup again, but the same thing happened. Filly went 12 yards and stopped. This time Alec was holding on so he wouldn't fall off. To this day Alec calls Filly "12 Yards."

It was June 5th and a beautiful night. Alec decided he would sleep out in the barn with "12 yards." Alec brought out his electric guitar. Alec started strumming his guitar, but he needed an ample fire to make it sound better. Alec had an idea. He put the cord into "12 yards" (Filly's) nostrils. Then he strummed the guitar. Suddenly a piercing note came out. Alec was stunned. After he unstunned himself, he played more notes. Alec played a full verse of "Rubber Saddle," and then he ran into the house. After he told his mother, he said that he was going to leave home and make his fortune. But his mother said, "No."

56

That night Alec ran away. He took off to Fleasburg. He found an opening at the Fleasburg Theater. Near the entrance there was a sign which read, "Manager—sixth floor." So Alec brought Filly up the steps because the elevator was out of order. As soon as Alec got to the manager's office, he knocked on the door. He waited patiently. Finally after five minutes his secretary came to the door. When she saw Filly she almost fainted. She said, "Come in." Alec and Filly walked in. She lead them to the manager. On his desk there was a sign that read: Henry D. Daily—Acting Service. Henry asked, "What can I do for you?" "Well, Sir," said Alec. "I would like to go in the singing business." Alec told him the whole story. Henry said, "I don't believe it!" Alec said, "Well, I'll prove it." Alec took his guitar out of the case. He put the wires in Filly's nose and turned the volume up. Alec asked, "What would you like me to play?" The manager answered, "I don't care." So Alec started playing "Rubber Saddle." After that the manager thought it over and then he said, "You have been hired."

That was in 1965. And 1965 was the year in which millions of American teens bought the hit song "Rubber Saddle." The record was so popular that Alec opened a factory called "Rubber Saddle, Incorporated" (R.S.I.). The factory made plaster replicas of Alec, his saddle, and Filly. They also made T-shirts and school notebooks (with pictures of Alec) and they set up the Filly Press—which published the best seller, "How to Make a Million with Your Horse," and a new magazine called, "Everything You Always Wanted to Know About Horses."

As we said before, that was in 1965. Now in 1973 "Rubber Saddle" has come back into business. In 1971 "Rubber Saddle" companies everywhere went out of business. But now in 1973 "Rubber Saddle" companies are back in business. And "Rubber Saddle" records are the biggest hit since the record "Snow White and the Seven Dwarfs."

One day Alec decided to go home and see his mother. He was sixteen and had a license and a car and a horse trailer. When he got home there was an old lady and an old man sitting on the front porch. Alec got out and asked them if Mr. or Mrs. Ramsey were home. "You're speaking to 'em, Sonny." Alec spoke up, "Mom! Dad!" Alec ran to them. They started to get up but didn't have the energy and fell back into their chairs. Alec helped them get up. They went into the house. They had some supper and then went into the living room to have a game of Crazy Eights. While Alec was getting the cards his father piped up and said, "While you are getting the cards, get the paper on the kitchen table. It's my will. I leave everything to you; even my deck of cards." Alec said, "Not yet, father. It's not time." Alec came back with beer and cake.

"Just like old times," he said. Mr. Ramsey said, "Alec, one more thing before it's time to go. We want to be buried in Filly's pasture." Alec said it was O.K. It started to rain and thunder. It was Alec's turn to draw. He picked up the four of hearts. Just then a big bolt of lightning came down—CRASH!! He shouted, "FILLY—she's out in the pasture!" Then he remembered, "False alarm. She's in the trailer." But Alec didn't see his parents. They were on the floor with the table on their heads. Alec said, "Oh, no. It must have happened when I jumped up... the table...it fell...Oh, no...the shovel; it's out in the barn." Alec dragged them out to the barn. While he was out in the barn the telephone rang. Alec heard it but he said, "Just let it ring." It was the neighbors. They called and called but Alec didn't bother to answer it. So finally the neighbors called the police. The police went to the neighbors. They showed them the way over to the Ramsey's house. When they got there they knocked on the door but no one answered. Finally they broke the door down. They went in and saw the blood all over the rug.

While this was going on Alec was just coming back from burying his mother and father. The police came through the door and saw him. Alec saw them, too. He took cover behind Filly's trailer, which wasn't very smart. There were four shots. Two missed and the other two ... they went through the trailer and into Filly's heart. When Filly fell over to the side of the trailer (the side Alec was on) the whole trailer along with his Toyota Corolla fell on his legs. Suddenly there was a bolt of lightning. It struck the biggest tree in the yard. It started to burn. Alec knew it would fall on them. As the tree began to fall Alec shut his eyes but to his surprise it fell on him.

****   THE END   ****

I need to issue a warning about this kind of "directionless" approach to writing. I have visited many classrooms in which the teacher has written on the blackboard or in the writing activity area the instruction to "write a story, play or poem." My experience with that form of open-endedness is that unless you have a good deal of writing under your belt or are one of the elect few natural-born writers, it's an absolute mind paralyzer. (It is for me!) The ability to abandon assignments, starters, and gimmicks was the result of a year of exploiting precisely those techniques to the point where they were no longer necessary. A friend who does a lot of running told me that it's grueling until you build yourself up to the point of being able to run two or three miles without great discomfort. After that it becomes possible to relish the subtleties of the process, to experience its mystical qualities. There is a parallel in the build-up to self-sustaining writing.

The assignments of the previous year now became more of a security blanket than a central part of the writing program. Even some of the most prolific writers in the class experienced dry spells, periods when they were devoid of ideas. Maura and Sandy, two bright, spirited, and imaginative fifth graders organized a group of girls to recreate the imaginary worlds project of the previous year. They carried it through the completion of a book without any assistance at all from us, and the finished product was funnier and more lively than the one we had overseen.

Excerpts from Maura's and Sandy's work:

LANGUAGE

This is the Qausariland Alphabet which is called a sham poosmana:

A   B   C   D   E   F   G   H   I   J   K   L
M   N   O   P   Q   R   S   T   U   V   W   X
Y   Z

This is how to pronounce them:

A—LAL, B—Bup, C—cula, D—wimp, E—Wppp, F—fitico, G—goua, H—hita, I—AAA, J—Judy, K—kami, L—eli, M—momo, N—uni, O—ono, P—lupa, Q—qum, R—rogiga, S—sm, T—timtum, U—uta, V—viti, W—wi, X—xa, Y—ale, Z—zipa

DICTIONARY

wimp—AAA—cula—timtum—AAA—ono—uni—LaL—tiggiga—ale

The Word	How To Pronounce
	A
animal	lal—uni—AAA—momo—ala—eli
act	lal—cula—timtum
apple	lal—lupa—lupa—eli—whipa
always	lal—eli—wi—lal—ale—sm
army	lal—raggiga—momo—ale

59

B

big	Bup—AAA—gowa
baby	Bup—LAL—Bup—ale
bother	Bup—ono—timtum—hita—wippa—roggiga
bust	Bup—uta—sm—timtum
batter	Bup—LAL—timtum—timtum—whipa—roggiga

C

came	cula—LAL—momo—whipa
coat	cula—ono—LAL—timtum
cutter	cula—uta—timtum—timtum—whipa—roggiga
chains	cula—hita—LAL—AAA—uni—sm
chimpanzee	cula—hita—AAA—momo—lupa—LAL—une—zipa— whipa—whipa

etc.

SCHOOLS

The schools in Qausariland are very funny. They are made of layers of spit. They press the spit into blocks. The people who made Qausariland made up a pledge of allegiance. It goes like this:

Let us pray to
Mik and Fit our
Discoverors that
They had never
found this Rotten
Place. Let us pray
that it will disappear
and we would have
a Better one. Let us
When we die and go
to heaven that we
can sock them in
the Bean with five
hundred tangerines
let us cream them
and whip them up
like a pancake batter.

After the pledge of allegiance everyone gets ufy and starts stamping and grunting because they got all worked up. The second thing they did was to take the count to see who was absent. The teacher's name is Miss Tennis Ball. If we were bad, she would hit us with a tennis racket. If we didn't want to do our writing she would tell us to do it any ways and she wanted us to have the words bounce right down the paper. Our paper in school has Big lumps of wood that are still in it. Every time you try to write you rip your paper. That's why we can't make the words bounce down the paper. We have pencils that weigh 20 tons. That's why we do exercises. These are the exercises that we do. We have to lie down on our backs and put a tennis ball between our legs and bend up and grab it with our mouth. The other exercise is we have to hold a tennis court, all of us for an hour. We got rid of Miss Tennis Ball in one year. We made her swallow a frog and she croaked. We got a new teacher named Mrs. Gutless. She told us she didn't have any Guts. So you can't scare her. If you do you will make her die. She gave us a good and funny pledge of allegiance. She didn't like the other one. It goes like this. By the way, our teacher is very fat.

We love Qausariland
Because it has lots
of good things to
eat on it. We love
Mik and Fit
Because they
gave us their
Body for
our first meal
We love Qausariland
yipe yipe Ha Ha He

The End

We all got mad because we hated that pledge of allegiance. We scared Mrs. Gutless by scaring her the next year. We got the principal the next day. He was like a Prince. He wore a crown and he was always telling us what kind of a queen he would marry. He always read us stories of great kings and queens and knights. He made us write on one of those things that rolled up. We killed that teacher by stealing his crown and thorns that went on his head. He cried so much he drowned himself. After that we didn't have any principals for teachers. We had our parents. Our parents would come to the school and they would fight with each other because they all disagreed about how the school should be run. Mrs. Hairdum, Mitty's mother, made up a new pledge of allegiance.

61

It goes like this:

> *We like Qausariland*
> *But we don't love it*
> *because the schools*
> *are made of spit.*
> *And we like it*
> *because we have*
> *enough food. But we*
> *don't like it because*
> *we have so many*
> *deadly plants. And*
> *people who love*
> *Qausariland need*
> *their heads examined.*
> *We hate Qausariland because*
> *the children don't have any*
> *respect for their elders.*
> *We love Qausariland*
> *Because there are no prisons*
> *Because if their were*
> *Prisons then all our*
> *children would be in*
> *Prison because they*
> *killed all their teachers*
> *And we like Mik and*
> *Fit But we don't love*
> > *Them.*

THE END

Before we had our parents for teachers, our school was beautiful. It had orange peels all over the picture of Mik and Fit. We had mealworm eye balls on the floor. Our toilets overflowed and our sinks got so much stuff clogged in them not even Ajax could get it out. The sink overflows 100 times a day. We set the clocks at two when we get to school so we'll only have to go to school for one hour. There were pictures all over the walls. We had nice fluffy pillows till a guy called Fat Albert came to school and sat on them. When the stuff popped out the first graders would eat it. We had one teacher that loved our room. She said it was supercalifragilisticexpialidocious. She also said it was neat. The first day she came in she said, "Cool man, cool." Our parents fired her. They thought she was awful. We almost killed our parents. Now our classroom is ugly. It has no more mealworm eye balls on the floor. The toilets don't overflow any more. The sink doesn't get clogged. We can't throw oranges at the picture of Mik and Fit. Nobody throws up on the floor anymore. Now the kids are crying because the room is so ugly. One kid cried so much that he overflowed the school. That's how we got our new lake called Pewe Pot Lake; that was the name of the kid. This is what we had for hot lunch when we had teachers:

Ice creams for dessert.
Two steaks and two chicken bones for Mondays.
Buggy soup and turtle toes for Tuesday.
That is our favorite dish, but our mothers
never made it for us because they said it
wasn't healthy.
Turtle toes that fight your nose—supersonic
soup and matapats for Wednesday. We don't
usually go to school on Wednesday.
Masterpiece muffins and Metal Muffins and
Meadow Muffins for Thursday. Metal Muffins
are our treat for the week.
Friday we have nothing because that is starve
day in Qausariland. To drink we have shot
milk. Now that we have our parents for teachers
we have ten different kinds of vegetables
because they say they are good for us. One
day a kid said he was sick. So he wouldn't
have to eat vegetables, instead he ate chocolate
ice cream. So every day we act sick. That
is all I have to say about school.
THE
   E
     N
       D

THE AUTOBIOGRAPHY OF THE MOST FAMOUS DOCTOR IN QAUSARILAND

The most famous doctor in Qausariland is Doctor Robert Him. He was born and still lives in Macabean. He was known in his neighborhood as "Bob the Bore." When he was eighteen he got a friend so bored that he got thrown out the window. When he got back up to the room he had *just got thrown out of he said to his friend, "Why'd you throw me out the window?" His friend said, "Why do you think I threw you out the window? You got me so bored I couldn't stand it!" That night Bob Him thought over what his friend had said. Then he said to himself, "I don't like making people bored. It's so boring. Since I'm so rich I think I'll start a clinic to prevent boredom. I'll call it "The Most Unboring Place on Earth Clinic" founded by Robert Him. So the next day he started his clinic. He had an architect to design the building. And a building contractor brought his work crew and when the architect finished designing the building they started building.*

About a year and a half later the building was finished. During that year and a half Mr. Him bought all the furniture for the hospital. Then, since he didn't have a college degree in medicine, he leased the building to a doctor named Doctor Hide Jeckell, a very intelligent man. Then he went to the best college in Qausariland. It is called "Bomhowerr, Schwartz, Crousden and Malarki School of Medicine." After he went through the B.S.C. and M. School of Medicine he took a course at Macabean High on How to Prevent Boredom. Finally he was ready to operate his hospital.

About the best place to be in all of Qausariland is in the "Most Unboring Place on Earth Clinic." Whenever anybody gets bored, they rush to the famous clinic. (In fact, the most common sickness is boredom.) Some people have such bad cases of boredom they have to be rushed to the hospital in the Bored Mobile. The hospitals are the most fun on Saturdays because there is free entertainment all day. There is gambling in the operating room, wheelchair races in the hallways, bingo in the cafeteria, swimming in the bathrooms and smashup derbies in the elevators.

After Doctor Him had his hospital in working order, he decided to start teaching young people how to become unboring doctors. So he hired an architect to design a college. After the architect finished designing the college, the building contractor and his crew started building. A year later, the building was finished. Doctor Him said he would name it "The Famous Doctor Robert Him School of Medicine." To be able to be accepted at D.H.'s School you have to be able to mix at least ten different kinds of drinks, know how to play bingo, know how to swim, gamble, and operate an elevator.

64

STORIES AND BELIEFS

by Maura and Sandy

"The Bed Time Story"

Once there was a parasite. It was as big as a tree. It came every night to kids that weren't good and wouldn't go to bed. If you don't go to bed he will take your nose and pluck it off. And if you're good, the parasite will come and grant you thirty wishes and give you twenty big, fat juicy kisses. Then the kids go to bed. When they fall asleep, the parasite comes. The kids wake up and get their thirty wishes. Then they cut the parasite's mouth off so he can't kiss them.

THE
E
N
D

The Nursery Rhymes

Hickory dickory dock. The qausarie ran up
the rock. The rock split and he fell in a
pit. Hickory dickory dock.

Tack be nimble. Tack be quick. A boy sat on a tack and turned black. He screamed and yelled and ran down the street and lost his feet. Tweet TWEET TWEET.

Twinkle, Twinkle little zilch. I can't stand the way you belch. Up above Qausariland you look like a rubber band.

THE QAUSARILAND BELIEFS

The qausaris believe that when someone dies that they must eat him in one minute flat. If they don't, they think that the spirit of the person will come and take all of their hair. Then they'll have to spend $20 a week for hair.

"The Don't Kill Beliefs"

The qausaries believe that if they kill someone that they will have their egg cracked. Then they'll die themselves. If they kill someone and died themselves you could not be buried.

"The Don't Kiss Belief"

The qausaries believe that if you kiss you will stick together and you'll never be able to get away from each other.

"The Don't Hug Belief"

The qausaris believe that if you hug somebody your shell will crack. Then you will have to buy a new shell for $40.

"The Don't Beep Belief"

If you beep you'll smell up the whole of Qausariland. And if you do that they'll have to plug up your rear end.

We are too prone to consume writing activities like so much kindling. Kids took great pleasure in repeating the same format, exploring new aspects of it, feeling some special comfort in the predictability, just as they do in hearing the same story read to them over and over. I once visited the fourth grade classroom of a friend who had done "I Remember" poems seven or eight times. (Write a poem in which each line begins "I remember." Choose a theme like school or summer or a special place to build the memories around.) The work had not become hackneyed and predictable. On the contrary, the work gave evidence of deepening, of exploring new possibilities with each repetition.

In any case there were numerous ideas that were resuscitated, sometimes without prompting, sometimes at our suggestion. We had done a number of "trade-off" stories the previous year—writing parts of stories and passing them to others in a group to be continued. In one way or another this activity was repeated countless times in our class when it fit well into our encouragement of collaborative writing, a process in which the final written product was valued but the intermediate stages of social exchange, good conversation, and brainstorming were also important. Other formulas were often recycled as well. (Write a story in which parts begin alternately with the words "Fortunately" and "Unfortunately," or "Draw a magic garden or undersea place or outer space place where special things can grow or live or happen. Write an explanation of what you've drawn.")

Fortunately and Unfortunately
by Bebe Sargent and Sandy White

Once there was a thing named Harold Darossa.
Unfortunately, he was a mouse.

Fortunately, he had a home.
Unfortunately, it was in a race car.
Fortunately, he liked to race cars.
Unfortunately, he had to stay up late every Friday night.
Fortunately, Harold didn't have to go to school, so he could afford to stay up late.
Unfortunately, he didn't know anything.
Fortunately, the race car was going to be transferred to a private racing school in Kingdom Come.
Unfortunately, the car was going to the junkyard.
Fortunately, Harold got out of the car before the trash got smashed.
Unfortunately, the King caught him.
Fortunately, Harold beat him up.
Unfortunately, Harold got a black eye.
Fortunately, the King died and Harold became King.
Unfortunately, Harold didn't know how to be a King.
Fortunately, Harold had a cousin, Nixon Darossa, who was studying to be King.
Unfortunately, his cousin couldn't come til the 4th of July.
Fortunately, there was not a 4th of July in Kingdom Come.
Unfortunately, there was a 4th of July in Who-Knows-Where.
Fortunately, there wasn't going to be a 4th of July this year.
Unfortunately, when Nixon Darossa got there he took over Harold's life.
Fortunately, Nixon was getting old and he was so weak he couldn't boss anybody around.
Unfortunately, Harold was getting old, too.
Fortunately, one day Nixon died.
Unfortunately, Harold got very sick and he died, too.
Fortunately, they had a good funeral.
But, unfortunately, it was a very sad ending.

THE END

There were a few students in the class who never moved entirely beyond the need for structured assignments. Although there was not a single student in our class of thirty-four who failed to write regularly in quantities varying from modest to prodigious, it required different amounts of nursing and prodding to forestall entropy. I want to tell you about Regina to demonstrate that it's not the "dummies" who require special care.

I don't remember if I ever saw Regina's IQ score, but I don't need any supporting evidence for my contention that she was the brightest kid in the class. She is a tall, slender, dark-haired girl with a perfect-featured, classic Irish beauty. Regina is living proof of Terman's discovery that people of high intelligence are also healthier, stronger, more attractive, and better athletes than ordinary folk. (All those stereotypes of pimply-faced, cross-eyed, uncoordinated geniuses with which us betas and gammas have been comforting ourselves just don't hold up.) Regina is the fourth girl in a family of eight girls and one late male arrival. Her father is a Boston-Irish car salesman; her mother, also a Bostonian, is one of the most alive and energetic women I know, more youthful and vigorous after nine children than most teen-agers, as if some hidden battery stored energy from each child-bearing for later ones. Regina was one of the most prolific readers I have ever encountered. We had asked our students to keep a list of the books they were reading, and we had set an arbitrary goal of 10 per semester at whatever level was appropriate for each student. Regina's went up over 100 in no time. I often saw her on her bike after school, pedaling home from the library with books piled in the basket and strapped to the book rack. It evoked a memory of my determination to read through—in alphabetical order—every book in a small branch library on Eastern Parkway in Brooklyn. Technically, Regina's writing was impeccable. She rarely failed to score 100 on her weekly spelling tests and her grammar was faultless.

Yet there was a great void in that area that we refer to with such imprecision as motivation. Regina suffered from what would have to be called an atrophied will. She smiled, appeared happy but committed herself to nothing. Somehow the reading was a safe, passive venture, a process of allowing someone else's will to wash over you. And at home there were the horses that Regina loved so much. It was an enthusiasm her father shared, and he saw to it that Regina was faithfully transported to all the riding competitions within horse trailer-hauling distance and to lessons conducted by an Olympic rider. Regina could also talk with real delight about the antics of her little brother, awash in a sea of sisters. But outside these pockets there was a kind of stubborn disengagement, as if all the will that had been turned away from the outside world were invested in the struggle to keep the covers pulled tightly around her head. Her mother attributed a measure of the blame to a first grade teacher who had made Regina feel both strange and conceited about her precocious reading ability, whereupon talent and initiative went underground. That was certainly part of the story. The other sources of Regina's resistance remained a mystery to me.

68

Forcing the act of will that led to writing was a monstrous task, but when the process was done and the memory of it had faded, what remained was likely to be a work of real interest. Here is one of the first things I wrote with Regina, a collaborative "I Remember" poem in which we traded lines in a way that enabled Regina to take off from my associations rather than generating her own:

I REMEMBER

by Regina and Marv Hoffman

I remember smelling the gasoline exhaust from the buses when
I crossed the street on the way to school.
I REMEMBER BEING SPLASHED BY CARS ON A RAINY
DAY WHILE I WAS WALKING DOWN THE STREET.
I remember hiding under the covers when the air raid sirens
sounded, hoping the Germans weren't going to bomb
our house.
I REMEMBER HEARING THE FIRE SIRENS AND HOPING
IT WASN'T OUR HOUSE THAT WAS ON FIRE.
I remember the taste of my mother's raw cake dough. When I
stuck my fingers in it she would tell me I was going to
get a bellyache.
I REMEMBER THE TASTE OF THE MALLOX WHENEVER
I HAD A STOMACH ACHE.
I remember Phyllis, my first girlfriend in the second grade.
How excited I was to see her when I got into class every
morning.
I REMEMBER RUNNING INTO MY MOTHER'S BED EVERY
TIME I HAD A BAD DREAM.
I remember putting my hand to the back of my head and finding
it covered with blood. Before I knew it I was in the
emergency room.
I REMEMBER FALLING HEAD FIRST INTO THE BACK OF
THE CAR AND BEING RUSHED TO THE HOSPITAL.
I remember the smell of my sixth grade teacher's perfume.
Even now when I smell it on someone else, I think of her.
I REMEMBER TROTTING ON MY PONY, AND NEXT
THING I KNOW I'M SITTING ON THE GROUND WITH
MY PONY OVER ON THE OTHER SIDE OF
THE ROAD.
I remember seeing an old, old uncle just before he died. His skin

69

was all yellow and he looked so small on the bed.

*I REMEMBER BEING LOCKED IN THE CLOSET, AND MY
SISTER OUTSIDE IN THE BEDROOM LAUGHING.*

*I remember my sister pretending to go out, leaving me alone
when she was supposed to be babysitting. I screamed and
threw up.*

*I REMEMBER GOING AROUND IN CIRCLES ON A SWIVEL
CHAIR IN A RESTAURANT AND HAVING MY
MOTHER HAVE TO BRING ME INTO THE RESTROOM
SO I WOULDN'T THROW UP ON THE FLOOR.*

Inevitably we came around to trying to reach Regina through her beloved horses. We had become interested in exploring *special* places with our kids—places that had a certain magical aura about them, hiding places, places that were associated with people they loved. I don't remember what set us on that course, but it hardly matters; the idea itself is so compellingly evocative. Sandy, a fifth grader, had written an almost Walker Evans-like photographic tour through her grandmother's house:

MY FAVORITE HOUSE

by Sandra White

My favorite house is my grandparents' house. When you drive up the hill you come right in front of the front door. My grandparents call it the side door.

You go on the porch and sometimes you see caned chairs that are halfway caned. My grandmother canes chairs.

You look at the side of the door and there's a sign that says town clerk.

When you go through the porch you come into the kitchen. If you look straight ahead you see the washing machine. It's one of those old kind of washing machines. After you wash the clothes, you put them through the roller and into the rinse tub.

Then you turn to the left and you see the table. By the table is the wood stove. They only use the wood stove for burning papers and stuff. They use it to put hot pies and stuff onto. By the wood stove is another stove. In back of the stove is a gun rack.

Past the corner is a little pail where they keep wet garbage that you can't burn. By that is the sink. Over the sink is a shelf where my grandparents keep medicine.

By the sink is a door that leads to the pantry but the door is always open. (I didn't even know there was a door there until a few months

70

ago.) In the pantry they keep dishes, butter, mixes, peanut butter, etc.

When you come out of the pantry, there's a bureau, sort a like. That's where they put magazines. Next to that is the refrigerator. By the refrigerator is the washing machine. By the washing machine is a door that goes to the dining room.

You turn to your right and there's the telephone stand. There's a cabinet like in the telephone stand and it has magazines and crayons in it. Next to the telephone stand is a cabinet. It has silverware and stuff. There are two clocks on top of it but I think one of them is broken.

Right by the corner are three windows. In the windows are candle molds and plants. In front of the window is the dining room table. By that is another cabinet. It has about ten million packs of cards on it. It has a whole bunch of pictures on it too. There's cameras and film on the cabinet.

Across the room is a couch. By the couch is another wood stove.

We often pyramided our work by using a good piece by one student to stimulate other writing in the same vein. Regina read Sandy's piece and chose to write about her barn. "Chose" is hardly accurate. It was more the case that she decided if she was going to be obligated to write something it might as well be that. She was surly and resentful throughout. She was really mad at us for pressing on her with such determination, demanding some inner statement. We had enough presence of mind to keep her mother informed about what we were up to, even to the point of soliciting her advice on the wisdom of refusing Regina a grade in "language arts" until she had submitted additional writing. Her mother was willing to support this calculated risk because she too was worried about Regina's lack of engagement with school.

What emerged from this tussle was a work of fine feeling, which was helped along midway with a suggestion from Dick that she imagine the description was directed to a blind man, hence all the smell references.

MY FAVORITE PLACE

A Description—by Regina Rafferty

There are two big overhead doors in the front. You go in the door and to your left there is a lot of hay tied with ropes. To your right there is a big box filled with curry combs, brushes, mane and tail combs, ointments, and lead ropes. Up above the box is a saddle rack for my sister's bridle and for mine when I get it.

Over by the hay there is a bag of grain for the horses to eat, a lot of rakes, hay forks and shovels, grain bags, and barrels for shavings to put

71

in the stalls and a wheel barrow to put the manure in. Right when you go in the door there are two stalls with my sister's and my horse. Around the stalls are metal bars so that the horses won't bother each other. Above my sister's horse's stall there is a plaque that has the name "Tiffany" and a picture of a horse's head. Tiffany is my sister's mare's name. I don't have a plaque for my horse's stall, but I want to get one that says "Tessie" on it because that's my mare's name.

I like to ride a lot so I spend a lot of time with Tiff and Tess. The hay smells sweet like the grass in spring. It also has a sort of dusty smell. The grain smells like corn and wheat, oats and molasses. That's my favorite smell. Another smell is the smell of the shavings and the manure. They aren't such pleasant smells. Right outside the door to the left is the pasture. The pasture is about an acre and one-third big.

From here it was a short step to the transformation of the prose piece into a poem. Regina had been working on extracting found poems from printed material, a low risk venture, and now she could simply use her own prose as the source of found poetry. The inner work was done. All that remained was for Regina to turn her considerable powers of language on the material.

MY FAVORITE PLACE

A Poem—by Regina Rafferty

Two big overhead doors
in front. Walk in,
turn left. There is
hay tied with ropes.

Smell the hay—
sweet like the grass
in spring, combined
with dust.

Turn right—
a box filled with curry combs
brushes, mane and tail combs,
ointments and lead ropes.

Look above the box—
a saddle rack for my sister's saddle.
Look above the rack—
two bridles for my sister's horse
(and for mine
when I get it).

Next to the hay
a bag of grain waits
for the horses to eat it.
Its smell is like oats
corn, wheat and molasses
(my favorite smell).

Rakes, hay forks and shovels
stand quietly in a corner
waiting for hands
to pick them up
and use them
to clean the stalls.

Then the grain bags
and the barrels for shavings
to put in the stalls.
Then the wheel barrow
to put manure in.

Take a couple of
steps forward.
A stall
for my sister's horse.
All around the stall—
metal bars (so the horses
can't bother each other).

Above my sister's stall
a plaque that says
"Tiffany."
That's her mare's name.

Above my mare's stall
a plaque that says
"Tessie."
That's her name.

Right outside the door
to the left is
the pasture.
(That's where I spend most
of my time.)

Both these pieces were read and admired by kids, teachers, and
parents, and it would be nice to report that a turning point had been

reached, though Regina was too cool to let on in any notable way that anything had changed. But it had. Dick engaged her in a project that had its roots in what we had learned from John Hawkes and Jonathan Baumbach about the "Voice" project at Stanford University, an experimental freshman English program that attempted to impart an understanding of the variety of literary voices and how they are achieved [see Baumbach's account in *Writer As Teacher: Teacher As Writer* (Holt, Rinehart and Winston, 1970)]. Regina was one of the few kids well-read enough to have the literary sensibility to grasp such a concept. What she chose to juxtapose here is the antiseptic media eye and voice on the one hand and the voice of a surly, snobbish narcissistic actor, both perceiving and speaking about the same events. This project required a lot of one-to-one attention and discussion en route, but what emerges is a work of genuine humor and sophistication.

THE TRUTH ABOUT QUINCY CAPRI

by Regina Rafferty

FLASH

WRTO Radio reports: Quincy Capri, the famous Hollywood Movie Director, met with reporters yesterday and announced that he was planning to make his next film in rural Vermont. "I need a change of pace," he said. "My life has been too complicated in the city. I want to find the simple life. Fresh air, a few close friends, and plenty of elbow room."

> The sixteen Cadillacs crossed the border into Vermont last night. In each Cadillac there was a color television, a telephone with a direct line to Hollywood, and fifteen pretty young secretaries to Mr. Capri.

FLASH

Quincy Capri says that he has never been happier. He says he loves the simple people of Vermont.

> In Vershire, one of the Cadillacs hit a chicken. Sam Sloop, the farmer, ran out to stop the caravan. Quincy Capri said, "Drive on! Oh, how I hate these country hicks."

74

FLASH

Quincy Capri is now driving in his little '65 Ford down Main Street in West Fairlee. "Oh, I love these small country towns," he says.

> *In West Fairlee, one of the Cadillacs ran out of gas. The caravan pulled to a stop at a local gas station, and it took ten minutes to convince the gas attendant that all they wanted was a tank of gas. Quincy says, "What stupidity, What a small run-down-town."*

FLASH

Quincy Capri has almost reached his destination, Fairlee. He is in the village of Ely now. He says he loves the small simple towns and is going to love his stay.

> *In Ely Quincy gets out of his Cadillac while his chauffeur is going to the bathroom. He looks around and says, "What kind of town is this! Why, it doesn't even have a movie studio or a supermarket or a shopping plaza. These people are crazy fools."*

FLASH

Well folks, Quincy Capri has finally reached Fairlee. He says he is now going to start to film his movie in two days. "This movie is going to be fantastic. Because I love this country," says Quincy Capri.

> *"Well, we're finally here, Mr. Capri," says his chauffeur. "Oh my Gosh! I have to make a movie here! This is going to be the worst movie I have ever made. Is this what you call an inn? They could have at least installed an elevator or an escalator."*
> *"Why, Mr. Capri, I thought you liked small towns," says the chauffeur. "I don't like small towns, I like big small towns."*

75

Quincy Capri is now staying at the Lake Morey Inn, the second best in all Fairlee. He is planning to make his movie in the center of the town of Fairlee. The name of his movie is "Slimey Snively and the Gold Robbery."

At two o'clock in the morning Quincy Capri called Room Service and said, "Where's the steak I ordered an hour ago? It should be done by now." The waiter explained, "I'm sorry, Mr. Capri, but as we've already told you, our kitchen closes at exactly nine." "Just remember," Quincy screamed, "I'm the famous Hollywood movie director and when I want service, I get service." Then Quincy Capri slammed down the phone. A second later, he dialed room service again. He said, "Now snap to it! I want my steak! Now! Medium rare! And if it's not perfect, I'll sue." The waiter answered, "Yes, Mr. Capri, Anything you say Mr. Capri."

FLASH

Folks, I spoke personally to Quincy Capri only yesterday, and this is what he told me. I quote: "I'd like to find a small, one-bedroom cottage without electricity, heat or a telephone. Like I've already said I want to lead a simple life for at least one summer. Since this is such an important movie that I'm making, I'll need all the peace and quiet I can get without any interruptions." Yes, folks, it sounds like Quincy Capri's gonna make a great film right here in Fairlee, Vermont.

Quincy Capri got into his shiny black Cadillac wearing a dark suit and tie and started out on a little trip around the lake. His shopping spree started at red lodge. His chauffeur got out of the car and asked Mr. Chapman if he would like to sell his cottage for half a million. The chauffeur yelled back to the car to ask if Quincy wanted to get out to see the house. "Why bother. Just ask him if it has a heated swimming pool, a sauna, electric heat, and a telephone in each room." Mr. Chapman said, "Sorry, Mr. Capri, but we don't even have heat. This is just a summer cottage." Quincy said, "Next."

The next house was the home of Mr. & Mrs. William W. Williams, Jr. "This time I'll go to the house," said Quincy. He went up the walk and knocked on the door. Mr. W.W.W. answered the door. "Good afternoon," he said. Quincy Capri said, "You'll sell your house to me for a million dollars, won't you?" W.W. Williams answered, "That depends on who you are and what you want to use it for." "What an insult," Quincy said, "Everybody knows who I am." And with that he got in his car and drove off. Mr. W.W. Williams said, "Well, here's one somebody who doesn't."

Quincy Capri's next stop was the Gehagans. The ·chauffeur said, "This place looks like it would suit you, why not stop here?" Quincy said, "It does look nice. I do find nice places, don't I." His chauffeur gave him a cold look.

Mr. Gehagan walked out on his porch to greet the Cadillac. Quincy got out of his car and said, "Out of the way! I'm Quincy Capri, famous

Hollywood movie director. I'd like a martini." He sat down in the livingroom in Mr. Gehagan's favorite armchair. "With plenty of gin," he added.

Mr. Gehagan poured a drink for Quincy and himself and said, "Ok. Now, what else do you want? All my furniture?" Quincy said, "More than that, I'm going to buy your house for a million dollars. Is there a phone in every room?"

Mr. Gehagan said, "You are, are you," and he threw his drink at Quincy and threw him into the fireplace. Mr. Gehagan said, "And here's a couple of lighted matches for good measure." And he threw some gas on him too, for good measure. Quincy's last words, before he went up in flames, were "You really burn me up."

FLASH

Ladies and Gentlemen, we interrupt this program to bring you the tragic news that Quincy Capri has just died from drinking on the job and heartburn. He was in Fairlee working on his latest movie and living his simple life and having a couple of drinks with the close friends he has made in this little town over the summer. All over Fairlee people are mourning his sudden death. Funeral services will be held at one o'clock Tuesday, three days from today, at the Fairlee Congregational Church.

Only one poor old man came to Quincy Capri's funeral. When they put him in the ground, he knelt down in prayer and muttered, "Halleleujah!"

For most of the kids the writing process fell somewhere between the poles of complete autonomy and helpless dependency. Most characteristically, a student who was between ideas and was not interested in repeating old projects and formulas would come to the teacher for a brainstorming session. Sometimes there was a lot of random talk before something would surface that might be a lead to a new writing project. Just as often one of us was ready with an idea for someone who had run dry, something that grew naturally out of other work the student was involved in. For example, Larry had been reading a book of Greek myths with great absorption, and Dick proposed that he write a play about a character he was intrigued by. The result was *Prometheus*.

PROMETHEUS

a play by Larry Farnham
SCENE I

Jupiter: *So, Prometheus has gone on another of his trips down to the bottom of the mountain. Why doesn't he ever stay here?*

Juno: *Prometheus is different. He is very interested in the people on earth. Ever since he created them he has been down there every day. They're like his children to him.*

Jupiter: *But why does he always have to spend his time with those so-called people? They're so little and tiny and funny looking, and they're so dirty and they have that funny smell.*

Juno: *Well, maybe he likes them and likes to stay with them.*

Jupiter: *Well, he doesn't have to go down every day. Anyway, I planned to have a meeting of all the gods at two o'clock. It's one thirty now. It's ridiculous. He'd better get here soon if he knows what's good for...*

    (A door opens and Prometheus walks in)

Prometheus: *Greetings, Juno. Greetings, Jupiter.*

Juno: *Oh, hello, Prometheus. We were just talking about you.*

Jupiter: *(Under his breath) Boy, were we talking about you! Well, what brings you back here? We didn't expect you back so early. In fact, we're surprised to see you at all! You seem to spend more time with people than you spend with us here.*

Juno: *We do miss you Prometheus.*

Prometheus: *I came here to ask you a favor. You know, it's getting pretty cold down there on earth. The wind blows and it's*

	chilly. Sometimes white ice falls from the sky. The people have to wrap themselves in animal skins to keep warm and sometimes, if they can't get enough skins, they freeze.
Jupiter:	*So what! Let 'em freeze!*
Juno:	*Let him go on with his story, Jupiter.*
Prometheus:	*Yesterday, I went to visit Demeter, the Goddess of Spring. I asked her to make it warm all the time on earth. But she refused. So, that's why I'm here, to ask you. Can you help me?*
Jupiter:	*I don't know. What kind of help do you want? Why are you bothering us with this business? Why spend your time thinking about those smelly things on earth?*
Juno:	*Yes, Prometheus. Why not just take off your shoes and sit down and relax with us. Have a glass of wine, the best of everything is right here.*
Prometheus:	*But please. I need your help. People are going off, one by one. Before you know it there aren't going to be any left. I can't let that happen.*
Jupiter:	*OK, OK, OK, Prometheus. I heard that story already. What do you want me to do?*
Prometheus:	*You could let me take fire to the people.*
Jupiter:	*Fire? Now listen here, Prometheus! I run a business with the gods. People could never be trusted with fire. Before you know it, they would let the fire get out of hand. They would burn up themselves and us along with them. Only the gods can be trusted with fire—and I am beginning to wonder about you, Prometheus. Never. Out of the question.*
Juno:	*Well, Prometheus. You know he's right, in a way. Fire is a very dangerous and powerful thing. Your people already are famous for getting into fights and wars—suppose they used fire. Suppose they started throwing it around. So far your people haven't bothered us because they only have stones and sticks and a few wooden axes. They can't harm much. But with fire...!? Jupiter, maybe we could arrange to get them some extra blankets.*
Jupiter:	*No, I think Prometheus has gone too far this time. He's*

80

off his rocker. He simply must stop thinking about these people on earth. You may go, Prometheus.

— *CURTAIN* —

SCENE II

TIME: THE NEXT DAY
PLACE: VULCAN'S FORGE
CHARACTERS: Vulcan and Prometheus

(Throughout this scene, Vulcan shows that he is very smart, and knows exactly what Prometheus is up to. As Prometheus walks in, Vulcan is hammering a sword for Jupiter.)

Prometheus: Hi, Vulcan. How's things going?

Vulcan: *(Looking up from his forge for the first time)* Oh, hello Prometheus. I didn't hear you come in. I've been expecting you.

Prometheus: You what?

Vulcan: Oh, you know what I mean, Prometheus. I know why you're here.

Prometheus: But, Vulcan. I just wanted to drop by and say hello.

Vulcan: Sure you did. Listen, don't think you're going to try to fool me, Prometheus. I know what you're here for.

Prometheus: All right, Vulcan. I didn't just come by to say hello. I came to, to...

Vulcan: You came to ask me for fire, right?

Prometheus: Well, yes I did.

Vulcan: Don't you know the rules? Remember what happened to the last god who made Jupiter angry? He was chained to a rock and threatened with an eagle flying around his head. You know, Prometheus, that could happen to you.

Prometheus: Well, I have to do something or they'll all die. Those poor people down on earth. They're going off by the dozen.

Vulcan: You really care for those poor people, don't you, Prometheus.

Prometheus: Yes, I do.

Vulcan: Well, I can understand that. But I can't help you. Rules are rules. And I depend on Jupiter for all my fuel, don't forget. I couldn't go against him.

81

Prometheus:	Well, I guess you're right, Vulcan. I do care too much about everything. I just get too involved in everything. This time I think you're right. I think I'll go home and relax and read a book.
	(starts to walk toward the door) So long, Vulcan.
	(Looks back) Hey! That's a pretty nice sword you're making. Who's it for, if you don't mind my asking?
Vulcan:	I'm making it for Jupiter. It's a present for him for being top god for all these centuries.
Prometheus:	That's pretty nice. I've never seen a sword quite like it. That's a new design, isn't it?
Vulcan:	Yes, in fact it is.
Prometheus:	And look at that handle. It's really quite amazing the way you have put those jewels on it.
Vulcan:	Thank you, Prometheus.
Prometheus:	Could you bring it over here to the light where I could get a better look? It's kind of hard to see it from here.
Vulcan:	Sure, Prometheus.
Prometheus:	*(He looks at the sword in the window)* Oh, this is wonderful. The best sword I've ever seen. But, I still can't quite see it that well. Vulcan, could you move over there just a bit? You're in my light.
Vulcan:	Well, I put a lot of work into that sword. I hope Jupiter likes it.

(Vulcan leans down and starts to work on the sword again. Prometheus leans down to get some fire. Vulcan pretends not to see him. Prometheus gets it and heads for the door.)

| Prometheus: | Goodbye, Vulcan. |
| Vulcan: | I'll see you, Prometheus. *(Under his breath)* Good luck, sure hope you don't get burned. |

(Curtain)

SCENE III

(At the bottom of Mount Olympus. The Castle of the Gods can be seen at the distance at the top of mountain. Prometheus is in the middle of the stage, lighting a fire. A few adults and some children are watching from as far away as they can get.)

1st voice:	*What is he doing?*
2nd voice:	*I don't know. It looks like he carried a piece of the sun in his hand.*
3rd voice:	*I wonder what he is doing?*
1st voice:	*It looks like he's trying to make that piece of sun into a bigger piece of sun.*
2nd voice:	*Look at the clouds he is making. There, it's going up.*
3rd voice:	*Do you suppose that's how the gods make clouds?*
1st voice:	*But that doesn't smell like clouds.*

(Prometheus notices them and motions to them to come. One man walks slowly across the stage to the fire. He puts his hand down into the fire, and pulls it out quickly. He yells and starts jumping around.)

Prometheus:	*Don't put your hands in it. Put them over it like this. Now you try it.*

(Then the biggest one tries it again. This time he just puts his hands over it. Smiles and motions to the others to come try it.)

1st man:	*It's warm. It's just like summertime.*

(The other people start coming over to the fire. They put their hands down, too. Soon everyone is standing around the fire keeping warm.)

Chapter 6

A SPECIAL CASE

There was only one lapse during that second year from our avoidance of full-class assignments, and that's a story that deserves a special telling. It begins, as do so many things of the spirit, with money. We were all near broke, living on half-salaries and therefore constantly on the lookout for ways of making money. We jumped at the opportunity to teach an extension course through the University of Vermont on writing with children. We were also lonely and isolated, very much in need of the stimulation of other active, engaged teachers. It's an all-too-familiar affliction for serious teachers in many school systems. There were three other teachers at our school, but for various reasons we couldn't get close to any of them.

It was one of those courses that would be canceled if ten people didn't enroll, and the first night's session was given over to a lot of frantic phoning by the eight people who showed up to friends who might be interested enough to swell the ranks to ten. Our survival assured, we settled down to seven or eight weeks of writing together, describing what we had tried with our classes, and reading examples of students' work. Reading and writing with teachers in this kind of framework is often a very moving experience for me. One sees people being surprised at themselves and what they've created, and no less surprised by one another, unable from that point on to approach the others without a special feeling of respect for what is within them. I suspect that the complex of emotions—surprise, delight, pride, respect—elicited by the writing is as significant for teachers who are approaching the writing process with children as the specific techniques themselves. Adults have to see writing as a source of pleasure before they can convince children that it's fun.

The last five weeks of our course we devoted to working on a new project together. The great danger in presenting your ideas and activities in a course format is that they will simply be parroted, that what are intended as examples of possibilities will be confused with the *style* they attempt to exemplify. To counteract this tendency, we decided to experiment with new activities together. The class chose to focus on the fact that although there was an abundance of ideas for stimulating "creative" writing, there was a real paucity of ways to engage children in realistic descriptive writing. So from week to week we each concocted our own activities, tried them out, wrote journal accounts of what happened, gathered up examples of student work, and traded the ideas around to try out in each other's classrooms. It's the closest I've come to experiencing something approaching the written descriptions of teacher-directed curriculum development in British teacher centers. (I am planning to describe the ideas that resulted in a separate article.)

Our part in the process was similar to that of the other teachers. We tried assignments each week and brought the results to our course. It was a bizarre contrast to our normal writing circus, this narrowing down to a single writing activity in which everyone participated. It was so out of character for us that I think the kids actually enjoyed it, much in the way I've noticed with increasing frequency that children in activity-centered classrooms without tests or grades find workbooks intriguing. Stripped of all the connotations of rating, pressure, competition, there is a gamelike quality in working your way through the prescribed task that can be very soothing and comforting. We had also told the kids about our writing course and were honest with them about needing material. They understood that we were doing *our* homework. (Our course met at night in our classroom in Fairlee, and the next morning the kids were always eager to see what the teachers had written or drawn. Sometimes they used the teacher work as a point of departure for their own work.)

So from week to week we were gathering the class together to do some of the following:

- Write descriptions of some child or adult who was known to most everyone in the class, without identifying him/her—a person riddle. I was especially impressed by the ability that some kids showed in fixing on a telling detail, one which brought a picture of a specific person into sharp focus.

EXAMPLES

JOHN:

From the black toe of his sneakers to the highest hair on his head he stands about 4'10". The cowlick on his head makes his hair flip out in the front of his head. His two front teeth make the picture altogether. When he runs his feet kick up to the side

85

of him. He is also a very funny person. He usually dresses in blue jeans but he likes colors that stand out. His eyes are huge. He walks in a cool manner. Whenever he speaks he always says something funny.

SUZETTE HAYWARD:

In the spring and summer she usually wears short sleeve shirts. On her forehead she has a mole. She has long hair down to her waist. She is tall. She is about 5'2½''. She has blue eyes. She has some freckles on her face but not too many. She has a mole right under her eye. She walks medium but she walks in long strides because she has long legs. She wears pants most of the time, except on Sundays. She wears sneakers, too. She is kinda chubby but not that much. She picks fights with the boys. She has blonde hair.

● Sit in a large circle on the floor of our classroom and write descriptions of our pet chameleon slithering about uncomfortably in this world away from his safe familiar cage.

EXAMPLES

"Chameleon"

by Darrell

A chameleon has four legs, five toes on each. On the toes are very sharp claws. It has two eyes that move separate. It has two ears which are just holes in his head. It can hear. It has scaly skin on its back and stomach. When it is hungry it is speckled. It has a tail that can break off if he loses a fight but it does not hurt him.

If you look straight at his head it looks like an ostrich or a bird. It is very hard for a chameleon to see straight. His mouth looks like a snake. If you drop him he lands on his feet. He walks in a pattern.

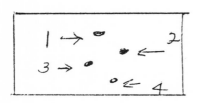 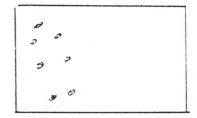

REGINA:

The chameleon is green most of the time, but to camouflage himself he turns different shades of green and brown. His legs are scaly and he has five toes on each foot that have little suction cups and claws on them. He has a long pink tongue that he coils up in his mouth. His stomach is a pale white with brown speckles. On each side of his head he has two little holes that are his ears. His skin seems to be made up of tiny octagons. His eyes don't have eyelids that close like a person's. The eyelids close from the bottom and the top. The one we're looking at has a broken off tail that is black on the end. There is a beige line down the middle of his back and all the way down his tail. His head moves in almost every direction imaginable. His eyes are on the side of his head, so when he looks at something he has to turn his head. When he jumps from one place to another, if he misses he always seems to flip over and land right side up. His head is almost the exact shape of a snake's head. He breathes about twenty-six times in a minute.

BRENDA:

The color of a chameleon is either green or brown. The skin is scaly but it is smooth, not slimy or wet. His skin is either brown or green on top and he has a white belly. He has four feet. There are five toes on each foot. Yes, he does have claws. They walk in a rotating way. His eyes are very beady and black. Their eyes move very much like horses. They cannot see in color. They have little holes in the side of their heads for ears. They have nostrils in the front of their faces. They can tip their heads back almost to a ninety degree angle but they have to turn their heads to see a mealworm in front of them. His head is shaped like a horseshoe with bumps on it. They eat mealworms, flies and other insects. They have pink mouths and long pink tongues. They have little ridges along their backs.

● Write depositions attesting to what they saw when two strangely clad bandits broke into our room and snatched from my hands a dimly seen statue. This activity, which blossomed into a day-long courtroom trial, grew out of my memory of some old University of Chicago psychological experiments on the unreliability of courtroom witnesses and was intended to demonstrate how many coexisting realities are possible.

87

EXAMPLES

DAVID SMITH:

Mr. Hoffman took the nude sculpture out of his bag, put his bag on the floor, and held it in his left hand. Suddenly the door opened. Two persons ran in. One yelled, "Hold it!" I don't know which one it was. One had a banana and was holding it like a gun. One had a goldish-colored hardhat and orange brownish hair, and he dropped a screwdriver and hurriedly picked it up. The other one had brownish hair. I couldn't tell what kind his hat was, but I think it was black. I couldn't tell either face from where I was sitting from.

SCOTT:

First crook: low voice; long, white hair about down to his shoulders. About 5'5". Very strong. Brown hat; red, old ragged shirt. Brown torn pants. Blue and white sneakers (Keds). A fake beard. Very stupid. Weighs about 122 lbs.

Second crook: Big red hat. Ragged green shirt. Brown wig down to his shoulders. Ragged pants. Big brown fake beard. About 5'7 or 8". Weighs about 190 lbs. Has strong legs and arms.

It happened in the middle of the room. The time was about 11:10 in the morning. Victim was not hurt. Object stolen was a wood carved eagle. The crime took about 3 seconds. Crooks are not found yet. The day is May 23, 1973. Victim has blue shirt, brown pants, glasses, is about 5'5" and is very smart.

LARRY FARNHAM—EYE WITNESS

Scene of Crime   *Wednesday, May 24, 1973*

A man standing in middle of room about 5'3", 160 lbs., dark hair, glasses, blue shirt, brown pants and black tie, shoes. At approximately 10 past 11:00, walking around with strange looking object. Looks like a sculpture of a bird. When two weird looking guys come screaming in—one with brown hair and a beard, gray hat and baggy grayish white pants, holding a banana, shouting, "I got him! I got him!" They were both about five feet tall. I couldn't get a good look at him but he had baggy pants, too. One of them was carrying an extremely dangerous weapon—a screw driver—which he dropped and picked up

88

again. Be careful; they are dangerous. If you see them, please notify your F.B.I.
   Thank you.

P.S. By the way, they took the bird. No harm done to the victim.

The whole interlude of assignment writing was odd and affecting, a nostalgic little reminder of where we had begun almost two years earlier with many of these same kids, and from which we had departed so drastically.

Chapter 7

A MORE "TYPICAL" DAY

A more typical writing period, one of two or three scheduled on a particular day for the Resource Center, would look like this. There are between ten and twelve students who have listed writing for this period on their personal schedules. A few other students have chosen to bring their math work or the tape recording of Eskimo stories into the Resource Center because they find it more comfortable to work in its carpeted, tie-dye-hung atmosphere. Three girls are huddled together against the wall under the typing platform, their knees high, their sloping legs serving them as writing tables. Each is writing her own story or play, but they spend a disconcerting amount of time talking, whispering, giggling; yet somehow by the end of the week the pages have mounted up and all that irritating "wasted" time has evaporated, leaving only the written distillation.

Above their heads a boy is on his knees in front of the low typewriter table, trying to peck out a recently completed story on one of the old Western Union office Underwoods we found at an auction. In all likelihood he will get fed up with his frequent errors, tear the sheet out of the typewriter, start again, and repeat the same frustrating process, in the end contenting himself to wait until Dick can type a finished version.

At one of the low Japanese-style tables we built the previous year two boys are reading a recently completed section of a play, on which they are collaborating, to Nick, our student teacher, who listens intently, weighing the comments he will make when they are done to insure that his remarks are neither too critical nor so vague as to be empty of suggestions for improvement or expansion. When Nick moves off to look in on someone else, they will return to their gentle tug-of-war over what the next scene should look like.

Dick is seated at his typing table near the middle of the Resource Center, surrounded by mountains of writing folders that are lying in disarray since their owners have rummaged through them this morning in search of their current work. Dick is in the middle of a collaboration with a student that involves an exchange of letters between a mad scientist (the student) and an irate enemy of the Doctor's (Dick). Dick is typing a reply to the doctor's latest ranting while the student peers over his shoulder to watch it take shape. A girl is also looking on, waiting for a few minutes of Dick's time. She has finished a story and needs some ideas for her next project.

In the corner of the Resource Center into which our miniature stage is nestled, several girls are rehearsing a play they have written that they would like to present during our Friday afternoon open reading, one of several opportunities the kids have to enjoy one another's work. They have waited for weeks for somebody to get around to typing up their script, a copy of which each now clutches with a dramatic air of self-importance. Although my primary responsibility this morning is for overseeing the science activities that are going on in the adjoining room, I slip in from time to time to listen to the rehearsal and to offer my most Bergmanesque comments on emphasis and intonation.

There are also two or three students who are more invisibly absorbed in their own private project. Some are working at tables, others have sought out a hiding place where they can enjoy one of the rarest commodities of an elementary school classroom—privacy.

Sometimes this setup hums and glows in an effortless display of efficiency, and we sit back and marvel at the number of good things that are happening simultaneously. At other times the noise is unbearable. Nobody seems to be doing anything and what they *have* been doing seems so shabby and thin compared to what they're capable of. There are days when nobody seems to want to write, and although we can be more indulgent of those moods now that our relationship with the class goes beyond writing, we still tend to push a little too hard for *production*. When I think about how many hours of distracted attention, daydreaming, and snacking are hidden in the interstices of what you are now reading, it gives me some sympathy for kids' uneven rhythms of work and attention; but it's also true that it is the discipline of sitting down at a particular time each day and staying seated through the long bouts of daydreaming that has made the pages mount up.

I know that one doesn't weigh success in writing on butcher's scales, but it has to be said that the quantity of writing over that year was truly staggering. Five or six children wrote several hundred pages apiece, not all on a par with *War and Peace* but an impressive accomplishment in itself nonetheless. I can't think of a single child among the thirty-four who wasn't involved in at least one writing project of some significance (both by his/her standards and ours).

91

When I've talked to teachers about our writing program, they often ask me what we did with students who wouldn't (couldn't) write. *There was no one who did not write.* There were kids who were more difficult to propel and sustain in their writing, but there are so many varieties of subject matter and process (collaboration, dictation, individual work, etc.) that it is the teacher's failure of imagination, not the students', that most often draws a blank in writing, as in most areas.

Paul was one of the boys in our class who recoiled from writing with the practiced revulsion born of five years of being misunderstood by teachers. We were Paul's first male teachers, and one day in late spring a woman appeared on the school playground. She had come for an interview with the school board for the position we were vacating. Paul looked at her, figured out what was up and headed back into the building muttering, "Uh, uh. No ladies. I finally got a man teacher, and I ain't goin' back." Paul was active, physical, forever in motion. He pedalled his bike up the state highway from his farm to school every morning the weather permitted (and sometimes when it didn't), and during recess he often rode round and round in expanding and contracting spirals. The fields of Paul's farm were visible from the interstate highway, and some days on my way north I could see Paul pedaling madly through the ruts and bumps of a hayfield or proudly astride his father's tractor, "helping" with the haying or planting.

Paul's life was motion and machines. Words were of little use to him. He was a bright boy. He could read more than adequately, but apart from a few books on motorcycle racing, he had found nothing that spoke to his world. It didn't help matters that he was the youngest of five or six children and had been pampered and indulged in whatever limited way such indulgence could be dispersed in a hard working farm family of small means. The effect of this treatment was to stiffen his resistance against doing things *he* didn't want to do. He was a charming, puckish boy who would first refuse cooperation with a winning smile; but when pushed further, he would plant his feet, suck in air, and exclaim, "No, sir!" He would refuse to clean up when it didn't suit his mood, but if he had built a piece of furniture on our workbench that really pleased him he would dash about the room emptying wastebaskets, vacuuming up, and putting up chairs without being asked. The way to that kind of boy's heart is through his body!

Some time prior to this I had found in a bookstore one of the insane Dover paperback reprints for which we all owe some anonymous editor a cheer of thanks for having uncovered and resuscitated. It is called *Absolutely Mad Inventions* and is a collection of drawings and written descriptions of devices submitted by their inventors to the U.S. Patent Office during the late nineteenth century. It contains such marvelous contraptions as a privy seat made of rollers to prevent users from standing on it (it never occurred to me!), an automatic hat-tipper, and a coffin with a vertical glass bell tower that protruded above ground. If one were mistakenly buried alive, one could, upon awakening, summon help by pulling the bell-string, and someone above ground could peer through the glass to check one's condition.

Dick and I had used the book as a stimulus for having children draw and describe their own mad inventions, but the match never seemed better between man and material than it did when we presented this book to Paul and suggested that he might like to invent something that would relieve him of an unwelcome burden. Paul hated his milking chores more than anything and from that distaste was born the following:

The Super-Duper, Extra Special
Brand New, Improved, Mechanical
COW

An Invention by Paul Ordway. Patent number—#1111, 8888, 34356

Your troubles are over. All you have to do to get all the milk you'll ever need is to press four buttons. Here's how it works. Press button #1. This turns on the water behind the milk tank (O). Water flows up pipe (P) into (L) and then into the wonderful mechanical cow (A). Now push button #2. That starts the cow drinking. It also makes the powder come down chute (C). The mechanical cow's beautifully designed metal tail now begins to wag up and down; this mixes up water and the instant milk powder to make milk (E). Everybody knows what this is. This is where the milk comes out (D), into the pail that is getting filled (F). (G) is the pail that is already full and is going down the conveyor belt to get empty. (H) is the conveyor belt. It goes around in an oval from the mechanical cow to the milk tank.

(I) is the slide where excess powder that doesn't get used comes out.

(J) is a second conveyor belt for the excess powder. It takes the powder to pile (K).

(L) This is the pipe we already told you about.

(M) This is a pail that is getting dumped automatically by a special arm (N) that takes each pail right up, tips it over into (T) a hole at the top of the milk tank (O).

(P) is the pipe we already told you about.

(Q) is where the water pipe goes in back of the milk tank.

93

(R) This is where the extra powder comes out.

(S) is the pipe that runs to the dairy.

(T) Like we said, that's the hole at the top of the milk tank.

(U) That's where the milk pipe goes through the foundation.

(V) is the motor to the conveyor belt.

(W) is the house.

(X) is the empty pail that is going back to the automatic cow.

(Y) is another pail.

(Z) is another pail.

(1) is another pail.

(2) is the barn.

(3) This is where the pipe goes into the dairy.

(4) is the road to the dairy.

(5) this is the Theodore Aiken dairy sign.

(6) is the whole dairy.

(7) is the doors.

(8) is the end.

YOU CAN ORDER YOUR OWN AUTOMATIC COW FROM THE INVENTOR: PAUL T. ORDWAY. ADDRESS: FAIRLEE, VERMONT. COME AND SEE A SAMPLE OF THE AUTOMATIC COW AT THE DEERFIELD FARM RIGHT IN FAIRLEE.

THE AUTOMATIC COW IS NOT EXPENSIVE. THINK OF ALL THE MONEY YOU CAN SAVE BY BUYING THE NEW, AUTOMATIC COW.

Paul T. Ordway says, *"Friends, I've got lots of money by getting all that milk from my automatic cow and having it go to stores. I just sit down and watch TV, and play cards with my friends, and go to the movies almost every night. Sometimes I go out for a big plate of spaghetti and pizza. I used to have to get up and milk at seven, now I can stay in bed until nine. And on Saturdays I just sit around and watch the Osmonds. All this is because of my wonderful invention, the automatic cow."*

Mr. Richard Murphy says, *"It's all true. I've never seen Paul T. Ordway work, except to count all his money. He must be a billionaire by now."*

Timmy Grey says, *"The automatic cow is the greatest thing since 1962. (That's when he was born.)"*

Mr. Marv Hoffman says, *"I visited Deerfield Farm, and I say the automatic cow is the really greatest invention that's ever come to the whole world. It's pretty, too. You can get red, white and blue, or black with purple stripes, or you can pick your own color."*

DON'T DELAY!!!

You can buy the whole works—house, dairy, pipes, conveyor belt, and pails and the AUTOMATIC COW ITSELF for only $9,999,998 and 32 cents.

— OR —

For just the cow, pipes, tank and pails: $999,998 and 30 cents.
GET YOURS TODAY!! NOW!

It took Paul almost a month to work his way through this project, and when it was done his pleasure was as palpable as when he finished his bookcase. With the exception of several racing car stories on which Paul had collaborated with his friends, *The Automatic Cow* was his writing work for the year. It was not a lyrical poem about nature, nor was it an intimate personal statement of feeling. Yet it came from some place close to the center of *his* being and therefore it was sufficient.

Chapter 8

THE PLEASURE OF PARODY

Everybody has a favorite literary form. It may be poetry rich in natural observation. Or confessional, introspective autobiography. Or sociological examination of a community or group. Or writing bristling with word play. That does not exhaust the possibilities by any means, but it's a fair representation of the central thrust of the work particular writers and teachers tend to elicit from children. We have explored all these genres in our writing work with some success and pleasure. Often one form seemed to mesh perfectly with the style and interests of a particular child.

But we found ourselves turning to parody with increasing frequency. Nothing matched it for the pleasure it gave to the kids. It comes natural to most kids and, in fact, constitutes a good portion of the play and conversation of older preadolescent children during their out-of-school time: imitating teachers and other adults, particularly those who are "weird", i.e. distinctively idiosyncratic; mimicking TV commercials and favorite shows; making up irreverent lyrics to the pop songs that are in ascendance.

Kids are often surprised, relieved, and a bit suspicious about the opportunity to "make fun of" (read: parody) things in school. It seems like the kind of thing they're supposed to get into trouble for. But when you think about how weak and powerless children are as a group, how few weapons are available to them in their confrontations with adult society, it makes good sense to me to hold out the weapon of parody to them as a relatively safe and satisfying way of holding their own. It's a weapon that has its own dangers, but they're minimal compared to the repercussions of, say, open resistance to parental or teacherly arbitrariness.

Young children do an almost endless amount of role-playing of mother, father, teacher, doctor, etc. They use roles as a means of learning about, experimenting with, and coming to an understanding, of their world. It occurs to me that at a later age parody carries this process one step further. In order to parody an institution or a person or a process one must first come to some basic understanding of its essence. I remember hearing from a teacher who did a good deal of simple typesetting and printing with his young students that he was amazed to realize how well they were able to read, since they were having no difficulty reading the lines in their composing sticks that were, after all, upside down and backwards. There's an analogous process of transformation at work in parody, an ability to grasp certain elements of style well enough to stand them on their heads. A child's ability to create a parody contains its own built-in test of his/her understanding of the subject matter at hand.

Our exploration of parody began before Fairleee with Dick's initial work on the imaginary worlds project for T&W. Dick discovered that the social studies class with which he was working was united in its disgust with the textbook it was being forced to suffer through. He hit on the inspired idea of enlisting the students in the task of writing their own textbook about a nonexistent country. This text would duplicate the tone of the original and would preserve its structure—those ubiquitous section headings in dark type that read: natural resources, climate, the land and its people, commerce and industry, flora and fauna, etc., etc. The result was funny, insightful and, I dare say, therapeutic.

We used this same departure point in Fairlee. Here the villain was also a geography text, but this time of a more "hip" variety. The flimsy fiction on which the text was constructed was that a kindly old gentleman, owner of a private 707 airliner, spent his time inviting groups of children to fly around the world with him. As they passed over Holland he would exclaim: "Look, there are the dikes of Holland. As you can see much of the land of this little nation is below sea level, and in order to make farming possible...." The contempt with which the kids approached this text inspired the following introduction to their own text:

AN INTRODUCTION TO KAWINEE
by John and Lori

Our plane took off from Friendso, where we had just gathered 250 grapes, at 3:40 A.M. Ann said, "I'm tired." She turned around in her seat and noticed Mr. Wilson sitting with 51 martinis in his lap. He was tubing those martinis right down. Mr. Wilson was looking out the window with his telescope. He said, "We are now flying over Miami; all take note of the pretty young lady in the bikini. Bob pressed his nose against the glass and said, "Duh." Jane said, "Mr. Wilson, stop tubing those martinis or you'll get drunk."

Too late. Mr. Wilson was already drinking another. Mr. Wilson looked out the window again and said, "I wish I was the man with that young lady out there." Jane said, "Man, are you drunk. There's no man with that lady. That's a cocker spaniel." Bob said, "Duh." The plane left the land and began to take off over the Atlantic Ocean. Suddenly Mr. Wilson pipes up, "Hic. Is that a killer whale down there?" Bob said, "Duh." The pilot said, "This is the last time I'll ever fly a Sabena. We're running out of gas!"

Mr. Wilson said, "All take note. We're getting closer and closer to the water." Bob said, "Duh." Jane said, "Help!" Then the plane crashed. We were in Kawinee. Mr. Wilson said to the pilot, "You idiot. You spilled my martinis."

Our classroom storage shelves were crammed with other antiquated texts the school board could never bring itself to part with, although they had been of questionable educational value even when new. One of these battered old books had a series of illustrations that caught Maura's fancy. She and Dick decided that it would not bring down the wrath of the gods if they cut these illustrations out and used them as the basis for a new text. The result was a visual parody that comes close to Donald Barthelme's quirky commentaries on the Victorian drawings, which have been the core of several strange pieces in the *New Yorker* magazine.

ME AND HENRIETTA
by Maura Rafferty & Dick Murphy

Me and Henrietta retired to the country with our life savings. We bought the house of our dreams. It was panelled with people. There was lots of work to do. I had to shinny up each pole and dust off the animals, while Henrietta held a net in case I slipped. After dusting, we had to sleep on the floor, and, of course, we had to install central heating. Finally, our work was done, and we decided to have a party.

People came from all over. They brought presents and lots of good things to eat. We found our new country neighbors very attractive. But we were worried because at first they didn't seem to like us.

But then Henrietta told some of her favorite jokes. Soon she was the center of conversation. Everyone wanted to talk to her.

But I was still lonely. I spent too much time at the bar, dipping into the big punch bowl. The three women bartenders started luring me on.

101

My head started spinning. My eyes began to play tricks: our visitors began to look like animals: fishy birds and scaly dogs. They had to put me to bed.

Meantime the party was getting really wild. Maybe our house (with its new central heating) was too hot, because people started running around outside naked.

Henrietta was flabbergasted.

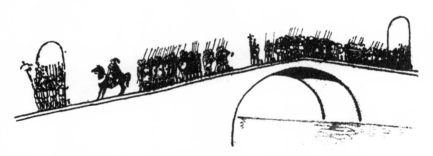

Someone must have called the police because, about an hour later, we heard bugles and horses and the sound of marching feet tramping over our bridge. The chief of police said, "Hand over all those naked people." Henrietta said, "If the chief of police finds out what's going on here, our reputations will be ruined."

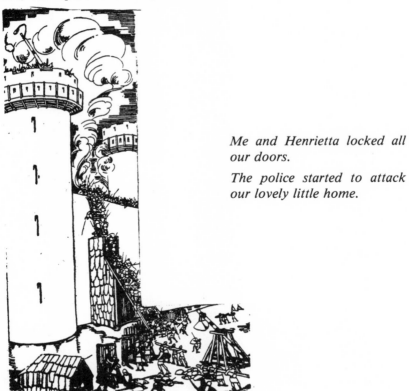

Me and Henrietta locked all our doors.

The police started to attack our lovely little home.

They got inside and treated us real mean. Then they set the house on fire.

Henrietta was outraged and miserable.

She screamed at the police. She got so mad she clawed and bit the five police sergeants.

But nothing stopped the police. Finally they smashed down the living room door. Our guests ran for their clothes. But it was too late. They were caught in the act.

They carried us off to a prison camp in the mountains.

Life in the prison camp was pretty hard. They made us pound rocks just for the heck of it. And we had to cook our meals outside over an open fire.

We had to live in caves, crowded in with another couple. We never had any privacy because the other couple had four noisy, naughty kids. We learned that all the other prisoners in the camp had had wild parties that got out of hand. Henrietta started to lose her figure and her beautiful complexion.

They kept us at the prison camp for three years. We thought we'd never get out. Then one morning a messenger with a torch came running through the field, yelling out our names. He told us to put all our rocks away in a neat pile, pack up our few belongings, and run with him to the courthouse.

When we got to the courthouse, they introduced us to the judge. The judge looked as though he had just fallen out of the clouds. He read from a big law book, and he kept on shaking his head and yawning. Henrietta kept falling asleep and I had to pinch her. His final verdict was, "Not Guilty....If you invite me to the next party!" Then he started snickering.

Henrietta said, "We wouldn't dream of having a party without you." And we were free at last! They carried us out of the courthouse as if we were kings and queens.

So once again me and Henrietta retired to the country with our life savings. We bought the house of our dreams. Henrietta said, "Let's not put in the central heating until after the party's over."

So we started to plan our party.

Our party was a great success. People came from all over, and there was lots of food and drinks. And this time, nobody got too hot from the central heating so nobody took off their clothes.

Only there was one problem. The judge said, "This party's boring!" And he sent us back to the prison camp.

Parody isn't reserved for objects of contempt. Anything or anybody with a sufficiently distinctive style is open to the same elbow in the ribs. We spent a number of weeks in our class viewing the twelve films on the life of the Netsilik Eskimos, which were made as part of the Educational Development Center's social science curriculum called "Man: A Course of Study." If you've seen the later re-edited versions of these films, you'll remember that they have a soundtrack and a standard narrative opening and closing: zoom in on an old man in front of igloo saying, at beginning and end of each film, "And that was the way things used to be." (The originals had no characters, no narrative line, and nothing more than the natural sounds on the soundtrack.)

All of us were entranced by the scenes of seal hunting, kayak building, igloo construction, etc., but from the second film on, we could hear the kids repeating the refrain, mimicking the old man, and finally ringing their own irreverent variations on the old man's litanies.

The playful parodying process was at work. All we did was acknowledge it and suggest a channel for it, rather than attempt to squelch it, as teachers often do. The result was the production of an ambitious movie, film number thirteen in the Eskimo series, which was made under top secret conditions by four boys who worked with us after school and on weekends for as long as there was snow on the ground. It was shown without explanation during a regular social studies period and became favored viewing for countless recess periods and lunch hours thereafter.

There was writing to be done in outlining and blocking in each of the film's scenes, but for me the film was glorious good fun first and, second, an unexpected glimpse into the extraordinary visual illiteracy of our kids. They were ultimate TV viewers, yet they had no sense of how the illusions on which they thrived were created—or that they were illusions at all! Here are some of the scenes that constituted their introduction to illusion.

SCENE: "The Eskimos break camp and set off on a grueling dog sled trek to new hunting grounds." Chris, the biggest kid in the class, owned Chocolate, the smallest dog in town. The museum in Hanover owned a lovely scale model of a dog sled, which we hitched to Chocolate. Hence, shots of Chocolate heading across the snowy tundra of our baseball field, lured (off camera) by tidbits of food. These intercut with shots of a determined Chris, wielding whip as he, presumably, rides along behind. Then the final denouement as camera pulls back to reveal tiny dog, tiny sled and huge boy headed across field in that order.

SCENE: "Seal hunters at the blowhole." Two hooded hunters set out across ice, find blowhole, dig it out, set cowhide alarm that jiggles as seal approaches hole. Many shots back and forth from one hunter to another to connote passage of time. Finally a sighting, a tugging, a great struggle, and up from under the ice emerges an old inner tube (some clever editing here). Hunters, full of mutual congratulations are seen in long view, trudging back to village dragging their prize. (These long shots made with camera stationed on roof of school, pointed in a direction that avoids views of houses, woods, powerlines, and so on.)

One final example of the pleasures of parody. Several of the girls became interested in the whole genre of do-it-yourself, how-to, fix-it books. I no longer remember how it came about. It seems to me that they puzzled over the absence of such books for women. In any case, what emerged was the "Do-It-Yourself-Manual" by Maura, Sandy, Cindy and Sue—a twenty-section volume for the ladies that included headings on how to fix your floor tile, sink, dishwasher, cracked mirror, and your face; how to get rid of bugs, take out the trash, buy the right kind of tomatoes, etc. Here are a few choice selections:

HOW TO FIX YOUR SINK

by Sandy

Sooo you got your sink clogged up again! What happened? Did your son throw up in the sink again? You really should teach him to throw up in the toilet. Well, let's get down to work. First you've got to make sure nobody's going to throw up. Then you get your utensils: ammonia, noseplug, turpentine, Top Job, vacuum cleaner, and a comb.

The ammonia and the Top Job is to set on the counter to keep your kids out of the kitchen. The noseplug is to plug your nose so you don't faint. You use the comb to comb your hair and make a good impression on your sink and if you make a good impression on your sink the stuff will come out easier. The turpentine is to slick down your hair to look better. Now you're all set. You turn the vacuum cleaner on and you suck up the junk with the vacuum cleaner and if it explodes you just take the Top Job and clean it up. You always thought unclogging the sink was hard. Now with the easy to do method there's no work or worry.

HOW TO PAINT YOUR WALL

by Maura

Sooooo you want to paint your wall. Now this is how you do it. Get some chopsticks, tooth brush, silly putty, ladder, umbrella. Use the chopsticks to make some Chinese food and eat it so you won't have to paint on an empty stomach. Use the toothbrush to scrape off all the old paint. Use the silly putty to stick in your holes in your wall. If there's any left, give it to your kids. Use the ladder to get to the top of the wall. Then you take the umbrella to balance on the ladder. Then you start to paint. Make sure you don't get stuck to the paint. If you don't use the umbrella, you will fall down and crack your head open. If you don't use the chopsticks, your stomach will growl. And if your stomach growls, you will get an ulcer.

HOW TO GET RID OF BUGS

by Maura

Soooo you want to get rid of the Bugs in your house. What happened? Did your kids leave the doors open or did they leave a window open? I know you leave your food on the shelf. Well, this is what you have to use: antiperspirant, rubber bands, wastebasket, and last but not least a sponge. First you get the antiperspirant and spray it on your underarms so if you get excited you won't sweat. Then you take the rubberbands and kill the Bugs one by one. Then you take the wastebasket and trap some bugs in the wastebasket. Then you sponge the Bugs out the door. Now after you do this you have to put on your thinking cap so you will remember not to leave your window open. Or your door. Sooooo next time you need to get rid of Bugs just look us up.

HOW TO PUT UP YOUR DRAPES
by Sandy

Soooo you got new drapes and you want me to tell you in my book how to put up your drapes. I just want to ask you one question: Why can't you keep your old drapes? I know your kid splattered paint all over your drapes. Well, let's get down to work. You will need a bikini, fish hooks, window cleaner, and a branch from a tree. Now put the bikini on. If you have a horrible figure you can't use this method. Now clean the window so everybody can see you working with your bikini on. When the men see you they will come around and offer to help. Now it's smooth sailing. All you have to do now is to tell them what to do. Now just tell them to take two fish hooks and hook the tree branch to the wall. Now tell them to hook eight fish hooks to the drapes and take the other ends of the fish hooks to the tree branch. If you have a horrible figure, catch your husband in a good mood and ask him to help you.
SOOOOO DO IT YOURSELF!!!! ......Almost.

Looking back over the examples I've included in earlier sections, it's surprising to see how many of them turn around some parodic center—John's plays, Paul's invention, the horse story, and others. It further reinforces my sense that parody is a natural, rich, and powerful focus for children's writing.

Chapter 9

LEARNING BY TEACHING

Dick and I had speculated often about how to go about instructing children in the philosophy of education. This subject matter is generally considered the private domain of educators, but the kids stand to gain at least as much from some understanding of why their instruction is organized in a particular manner, what choices were made to bring the current model into being, and what the alternatives might be. Now it should be self-evident that no self-respecting kid is going to sit through a lecture in educational philosophy. (I'm not sure any adult should either.) Such abstractions have to be approached through some form of active engagement.

What if we exposed our students to the *experience* of teaching and helped them look at the larger issues that grow out of that work. It was not a novel idea. Older children in multigraded classrooms carried some instructional responsibilities for the younger kids as a means of lightening the teacher's load. Other tutoring programs brought older and younger children together, often to demonstrate that the tutor's learning performance improved as well. We weren't so much interested in improving performance as in deepening understanding and awakening some beginnings of critical questioning.

We had the precedent of the previous year's project of making children's books for the kindergarten and having the older kids go in to read them during story time. The kindergarten was pleasant and safe territory for us and for our students, as it was easy to move into a regular format of sending students in to "write" (i.e. take dictation) from the younger children. Afterwards they would get together with us for postmortems—what worked, what didn't, the wisdom of giving choices, effective means of discipline, ways of motivating children—a pearl of philosophical wisdom buried inside each of these pragmatic oysters.

What we were most astounded by in the way our students went at the project was the variety of ways in which they demonstrated what astute observers of *our* teaching methods they had been. I don't know why we assume that kids are not aware of what's being done to/with/for them. Not so much in the sense of being clued in to modes of manipulation but being appreciative observers of the ways in which they're being handled, much in the same way a client in a therapeutic relationship may understand something of the techniques that are being *used* successfully to help him. In any case our students turned out to have a sizable repertoire of writing activities to try with the kindergarteners—the very same ones we had used to introduce *them* to writing. We had never reviewed these. The kids had simply filed them away mentally, complete with nuances in the manner of their original introduction. Of course, they parroted us too much, but it was a secure way to begin, one that would have given way to more personal teaching if the project had continued long enough. And the work they elicited was remarkable.

THINGS I WAS AFRAID OF
by Matt and Dominic
(told to Maura)

When I was little
I used to cry in the dark.
I used to be afraid of
    scary pictures.
When I was little
I used to be afraid of bugs.
I used to be afraid of
    bumblebees.
I was afraid of spider webs.
I was afraid of the water because
I used to think there were sea
    monsters.
I was afraid of sharks.
I used to be afraid of skidoos too.
I was afraid of robbers coming
    in the house.

LUCK

by Adina and Karen
(told to John Durgin)

What good luck there was going to
  be a party.
What bad luck a train is going to
  smash into the party.
What good luck they fixed the party.
What bad luck the train smashed into
  the house.
What good luck there was a surprise
  going on.
What bad luck that someone told about
  the surprise.
What good luck they didn't tell
  anyone else.
What bad luck a pick up truck hit
  someone at the party.
What good luck he was brought to
  the hospital.
What bad luck he broke out a tooth.
What good luck there was a dance.
What bad luck a cowboy ate all the
  candy.
What good luck they found a little
  gingerbread and a little peppermint sticks.

THE BEAR

by Larry Jewell
(as told to Maura Rafferty)

The bear lives in the forest. He lives with all the other bears. He gets mad at people. He catches little boys with his paws. He catches fathers, too.

He is wide and fat. Sometimes he is happy. Little toys are what make him happy. He has a couple of friends. His friends are nice.

He can swim. He goes to the fair. He's mad when he goes to the fair. He gets mad at the fair because he eats the children. His friends go to the fair to help him eat the children. He wanted to eat all the children up in one gulp.

116

The bear is black. He has big eyes. He has big paws. He shows that he's mad by his teeth.

He has a mother.

He climbs the trees to get honey. He doesn't knock down trees. The forest that he lives in is black.

He gets rrrrrrreal mad sometimes. He plays only with other bears. He likes to play with kids sometimes. But when he's mad he hates them. He goes on adventures alot. He has puppets. He has lots of string, too.

He likes to play with deer. The deer is very nice to the bear. The bear knows how to make letters. He likes to make deers out of wood.

THE END

THE ROCK

by Adina Hoffman

One day a little girl came. She picked some flowers. She was picking some flowers and she pulled so hard that she fell off the rock.

And a bear came and took her into his cave. The bear ate her because he thought she was going to die anyhow.

A farmer was so close that he saw the bear eat the girl. So the farmer made a garden on top of the rock so the bear would eat the garden instead of another person.

Then the farmer went onto the barn and hid to see if his garden worked.

THE GORILLA, TIGER, AND ELEPHANT

(A story that Karen and Dominic told to Maura)

Once upon a time there was an elephant, tiger, and gorilla. They had a tea party. It was the gorilla's tea party for his birthday. They think of the gorilla as a big strong animal. A pickup drove by with the elephant in it.

The tiger got run over. The elephant got mad. The gorilla started to eat a banana and he threw the banana peel on the ground and the elephant slid on it. The elephant got so mad he ran after the gorilla. Then the gorilla swung from a vine of a tree and knocked the elephant down. The elephant got up and slipped on the banana peel again. Then the tiger came along and he slipped on the banana peel. The tiger picked up the banana peel and threw it in the garbage. Then they were friends again.

117

They played jumprope and ring-around-the-roses. After that the gorilla fell in a box of crayon. Then the gorilla turned different colors. And the tiger and elephant laughed. After a while they decided to go for a ride in the truck. When the elephant got out he stepped on an apple and crushed it. It got all over his foot. They all ran off a cliff and got broken legs. They all kept hitting each other's legs and they would yell YOWE-YOWE-YOWE-YOWEEEEE! After that they fell down the bank on the side of the road and the ambulance had to come.

Dominic's elephant

*Car that the animals
took a ride in.
by Dominic*

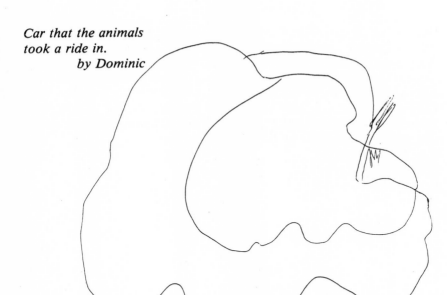

Karen's elephant

119

Two spiders.
     by Karen

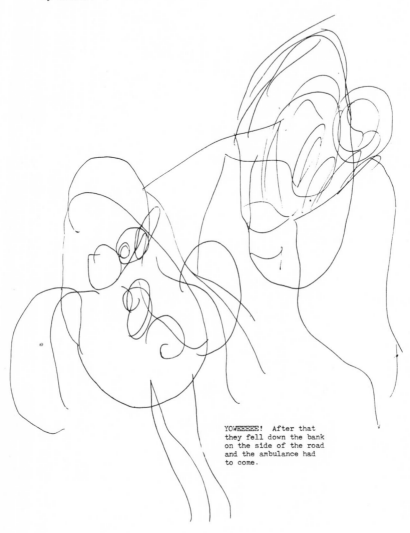

YOWEEEEE! After that
they fell down the bank
on the side of the road
and the ambulance had
to come.

This project proved to be an altogether wonderful way to bring
about some real growth as students, as writers, and as teachers for the
kids who participated in it.

Chapter 10

A PREMATURE ENDING

"For the time being I am content to argue that my approach is as consonant with certain deeply held conservative values—independence, self-reliance, suspicion of authority—as it is with liberal values. But part of me knows that this is not the whole story and that the local school board will begin to wonder, too. The political questions will have to be faced, and soon."

I recently found this concluding paragraph in a magazine piece I wrote shortly after beginning my work in Fairlee. It was a prophetic statement because we were gone at the end of our second year. We would have chosen to stay on longer but were not given that opportunity. I've read a number of teacher memoirs from Pat Conroy's *The Water Is Wide* on down, which recount how a good-guy teacher is assassinated by a Neanderthal band of administrators or parents. That's not the kind of story I want to tell.

On the contrary, I was surprised for two years that so many supposedly unsophisticated parents were able to lay aside their skepticism—and worse—and either come to appreciate what we were doing or at least arrive at a willingness to tolerate our presence. Sure, a lot of them were suspicious and a lot of them never did understand what we were doing, but they were not the mob of lumpen-fools who are usually portrayed as the undoers of good works.

Our opposition came from a small number (perhaps four or five in all) of parents and community residents who locked horns with us almost as soon as we arrived. To a certain extent they acted out of classical neuroses. They feared us as bearers of foreign contamination who would poison their children with sex, drugs, bizarre dress. It did not matter that we were in fact rather "straight" people. They saw what they were determined to see.

And they also saw something that was indeed real: our methods of teaching grew out of and fed into a philosophy and a complex of political beliefs that would change a community and a way of life our adversaries were determined to protect. On this score they were more right than even we were prepared to acknowledge. I am telling this story in a book that primarily concerns itself with "methods" because I believe that a lot of teachers have been rather imperceptive about the links between methods and the political statements they imply. Some teachers are bewildered by the "uptight" responses to their ways of working, which seem harmless to them, but there are times when style and substance *do* merge, when providing choices, emphasizing crazy imaginative writing over formal composition are the tip of an iceberg reaching all the way down to the work ethic and its role in the economic system, to compliance with authority and ways in which that is necessary to sustain an essentially non-egalitarian system, etc. I am not talking about the empty gesture that angry people often mistake for a political act—the nude picture on the wall or the swearing that says a literal and figurative "fuck you" to a parent or an administrator. I am talking about methods that are part of a cohesive and continuous fabric that is subtly yet consistently at odds with the institutions and the community that contains it.

In any case these four or five people sensed in an unarticulated way that we constituted a political threat. Their bidding was done by a larger group of community folk who simply didn't like "trouble," who would do most anything to root out sources of conflict. Who could blame them? We may not have looked so bad to them, but they wanted the hollering, the bitching, the arguments to stop, and if we were gone, that would be the end of that. No?

The process was simple. The superintendent, who had shown some courage in his past dealing with us but who also knew how and when to protect himself, simply did not send us a contract for the next year by the necessary deadline. When we first arrived in the district we had been promised at least a two-year stay, which he now had conveniently interpreted as an intention to leave after two years. By the time we had discovered what was afoot, recruitment plans were under way to fill our positions. The local teachers' association heard about our case and offered to do battle in our behalf on the grounds that no cause for dismissal had been shown, no notification of termination had been made. The principal was instructed to produce an evaluation of our performance for the school board. His own job was in jeopardy, and he lost it in spite of compliance on this count (though not because of us). There were some angry confrontations with the superintendent, with the school board, and countless evening phone calls with sympathetic parents and friends. And finally the decision that the battle had been joined with such bitterness that, even though we could have won on a technicality, we would never have worked there comfortably again. We decided to leave.

I can't say that we left behind anything that was capable of taking root and sustaining itself. The Resource Center was dismantled; the teachers who replaced us were uninspired at best and unhealthy for kids at worst. The teachers who remained at the school had adopted none of our writing ideas. But there were seven or eight children of that thirty-four who had really flourished during our stay in a way that would leave some impression. Although that impression was one they could draw sustenance from, it also made their adaptation to what faced them in their remaining years in Fairlee more difficult, in much the same way as Herb Kohl's Harlem kids in *36 Children* may have been harmed in their subsequent dealing with institutions by having dropped their guard with Herb.

In retrospect the original goals for change that we had set for ourselves seemed like the rhetoric of the sixties proposal and grant writers. The truth was that we had come to Fairlee to grow and to engage and mesh with the lives of a small group of children and adults, and we had done this. It's not the stuff of revolutionary romanticism, but as Joseph Featherstone has said:

> Careful work on a small scale is the way to start a reform worth having, whatever our grandiose educational reformers might say. In the end, you always return to a teacher in a classroom full of children. (This is the proper locus of a revolution in the primary schools.)*

---

*Joseph Featherstone, *Schools Where Children Learn* (Liveright, 1971).

Chapter 11

CONCLUSION

There's no grand summary statement. I've simply tried to show that a teacher with a deeper, more ongoing relationship with his/her children can do as well and better than professional writers in encouraging the production of large quantities of first-rate writing. I'm sure other teachers have done at least as well as we did but have left the reporting of writing experiences to the professional writers.

There is simply no substitute for a teacher who enjoys words, language, and imagination; who creates a structure that communicates to the students that writing is a central and valued experience in that particular classroom; and who is willing to devote sizeable amounts of time to writing activities, with the full conviction that they are as important as anything else the child does in school. To steal a metaphor from my wife, writing is a lot like nursing a baby. The more you do it, the more there is.

APPENDIX

ALL ABOUT LORI HAYWARD
by Lori Hayward

My name is Lori Hayward. I live in Fairlee, Vermont. My house is on Lake Morey Road. I like to ride horses. In the summer I take riding lessons at Lake Morey Stables. I ride a horse called Special K. When I grow up I am going to go out west and own horses by the dozens.

Right now I go to Fairlee Elementary School. I will go to Oxbow High School when I am in 9, 10, 11 and 12 grades. I am a happy, healthy girl and hope I always will be.

Signed,
Lori Anne Hayward

HOW TO RUN AWAY

I never thought things would get so bad. First, my mother got angry with me and started screaming. Then my father got angry with me and started screaming. Then I went to school and the teachers started screaming. I can't take anymore.

I am packing my suitcase. Then I am going to run away. I packed and then I went downstairs. My mother asked, "Where are you going?"

I told her that I was running away.

She told me that she didn't care. So I hitchhiked all the way to California and I stayed with my aunt.

A few days later, when my aunt thought that I was outside, she called my mother and I heard her

125

talking. She said that I was there. I had told
my aunt before when I had just got there not to
tell my mother where I was.

I started crying and went in the room I was
staying in and started packing my suitcase
again. My aunt came in and asked me why I was
packing my suitcase. I told her that I had
heard her talking on the telephone. I told
her that I was going to leave and go some
place else.

She told me that I couldn't be gone all my life.
I told her that I didn't care what she said.
So she called my mother again and told her not
to come for me. But while my mother and my aunt
were on the telephone, I went and got my suitcase
and left.

This time I went to my aunt Darlene's. She promised
that she wouldn't tell. So I said, "OK." We made
plans that she was going to take me swimming. Then
we could go horseback riding. I said, "OK."

We went swimming and had races and who could do the
best going off the board. She did the racing the best
and I did going off the board the best. Then we went
horseback riding and had a lot of fun.

Then we came home and my aunt asked me why I ran
away. I told her that I was sick of people yelling
at me and not listening to me. And I told her about
my other aunt and she said that she wouldn't tell my
mother that I was there and that she would let me
make my own mind up. I told her "thank you."

After a couple of weeks I got homesick and I missed
my mother and father a lot. I told my aunt Darlene
that I wanted to go home, so she brought me home
and stayed at my house for a while. After a couple of
days she went home. My mother thanked her for bringing
me home. And my aunt told her that I came back
on my own. And my mother was so happy. Me and everybody
get along now and I am very happy.

Cindy

126

WHERE WERE YOU WHEN THE YAWNING BEGAN
by Bebe

SCENE I

The curtain slowly comes open. Ompa Woompa is sitting in a chair. His eyes are closed. He doesn't say a word. Everyone in the audience should wait a little, expecting something to happen. But nothing happens. Then Ompa Woompa yawns—a great, big yawn. The same moment Professor Goodhart comes strutting onto the stage. He begins:

Goodhart: *Ladies and Gentlemen. Attention please. Attention, Ladies. Attention, Gentlemen. Quiet everyone. I am Professor Goodhart. I am respected and honored throughout the world. And this is my famous discovery, Ompa Woompa—the first man in the world to yawn. Ompa Woompa will now yawn for you. He is waiting for your attention.*
O.K. (He commands, pointing his cane at Ompa Woompa)
Ompa Woompa, YAWN!

Ompa Woompa: *(Yawns)*

Audience: *Yea, clap! Yea, clap! (Audience starts yawning; one person says this is ridiculous. This man is sick. Get him to a hospital.)*

Goodhart: *Ladies and Gentlemen. Please calm yourselves! You see this man is not sick. If he is sick then you yourselves are sick. You are yawning. Ompa Woompa is the first one to yawn. Together we have discovered yawning. We will be rich, famous, anything you can think of!*

(The people in the audience come running up.)

Person: *When do I start? I already feel like a movie star.*

Goodhart: *Now we must get started. Let's go home and get a good night's sleep. We will meet back here at 9:00 AM.*

SCENE II

Back at the Town Hall people are waiting for Professor Goodhart to arrive. He seems to be late. The people are getting angry.

Person #1:	*Where is he?*
Person #2:	*He should be here by now.*
Person #3:	*Him and that Ompa Woompa.*
Goodhart:	*Here I am. Sorry I was late. We must get started mustn't we? Now Ompa Woompa, let me hear your yawn.*
Ompa:	*hhhhhhhhhhaaaaaaaaaaauuuuuuuuummmmmmmm*
Goodhart:	*Now that sounds pretty good, but that's not quite it, ummm? And there's another thing wrong with you. Your eyes blink. I'll have to get you some special eye drops.*
Ompa:	*(patting Goodhart on the shoulder). You're a real movie star.*

(Ompa Woompa and Goodhart pause for a moment. He lights up.)

Goodhart:	*We better get home. It's getting late.*
Ompa:	*Yes, we must get some sleep. (He talks sort of drowsy-like) hhhhhhaaaaaauuuumm (Ompa falls asleep.)*
Goodhart:	*Ompa. Why did you have to fall asleep? Now I have to drag you out of here. (He starts dragging him out.) Goodhart says to himself—Now wait a minute. I have a better idea. (Goodhart goes into the bathroom and fills up a pail of water. Goodhart goes back into the office and pours the water on Ompa Woompa. Ompa wakes up.)*
Ompa:	*What's goin on? (Ompa is blinking and yawning more than he ever has before. And he is doing this so fast that he can't talk.)*
Goodhart:	*Where's the Doctor? (almost crying)*

SCENE III

Doctor comes running in.

Doctor:	*Where is he? What's wrong? Is he hurt?*
Goodhart:	*(whispering) Oh, another goober.*

128

Nurse:	*(comes lumbering in with a cane) Have you found him yet? (She says this in a squeaky voice.)*
Doctor:	Duh, I think I did, but I'm not sure. Does he have a mustache, long hair, and a little red visor?
Goodhart:	Yes, that's Ompa Woompa right over there.
	(The Doctor looks carefully at Ompa Woompa)
	Doctor, Doctor. Can you help him? Is he dead? If Ompa Woompa dies, my whole career goes up in smoke.
Doctor:	Don't worry. He's not dead. He just is sound asleep. What happened?
Goodhart:	It was terrible. It was about four-thirty in the morning. Ompa Woompa fell asleep on the floor. I ran over to him. I said, "Ompa Woompa, why did you have to fall asleep?" I ran into the bathroom and got a pail of cold water and threw it over Ompa Woompa. Suddenly he was sitting up, yawning and blinking and yawning and blinking faster than ever. Oh, it was a terrible sight.
Doctor:	Oh, I understand this has to be...unless it's... *(PAUSE)*
Goodhart:	Yes, Yes! What is it?
Doctor:	Oh, no. It can't be. That's much, much too serious.
Goodhart:	What's much too serious!
Doctor:	I've got it. It's, it's..Yes, that's it!

(Goodhart is getting furious while the Doctor is pacing back and forth.)

Goodhart:	What is it?
Doctor:	It is exhaustophobia.
Goodhart:	This is your last chance.
Ompa Woompa:	Yawn! *(Ompa Woompa just sits there smiling)*
Goodhart:	Haven't you got anything to say for yourself?

(Ompa Woompa just sits there smiling.)

Goodhart:	My career is over. We will have to say good-bye.

(Ompa Woompa just sits there smiling.)

(Goodhart gets up and helps up Ompa Woompa and they walk off the stage. Goodhart is feeling sad.)

in the same chair where he had been sitting.)

Ladies and Gentlemen. You haven't seen anything yet! I am Professor Ompa Woompa. I am respected and honored throughout the world. And this is my famous discovery—Goodhart. Goodhart will now yawn for you. He is waiting for your attention.
(He commands, pointing his cane at Goodhart...)

Goodhart, yawn!

(THE CURTAIN SLOWLY CLOSES)

WHAT IT FEELS LIKE TO BE DEAD

It's like you don't extend.
It seems like you don't have a face.
It seems like you don't have a body.
It seems like you aren't even there.
All you do is lay there and get skinny.
You eat parts of yourself, because you get hungry
*   and that's all there is to eat.*
Little black worms crawl into your mouth and into
*   your stomach. They eat away your insides out.*
Sometimes you throw up your insides and blood.
Then your eyeballs pop out.
Your ears explode and your eardrums come out.
The woodchucks eat the coffin away.
They put you in a bag after you die. It smells so bad
*   inside the bag that the bag rots away.*
People put flowers by your gravestone. It smells so bad that the
*   flowers wilt. It smells like a dead skunk*
*   with all the guts out of it covered with sour milk.*
White worms eat the rest of your body that you or the black
*   worms eat.*
Well, pleasant dying!

WHAT'S IT LIKE TO BE IN HEAVEN?

All this isn't all that bad because after you finish dying
you go to heaven.

In heaven they have Holiday Inns, indoor swimming pools,
outdoor swimming pools, horseback riding, color TV,
good food and anything you want and everything is free.
The rooms in the Holiday Inn are really nice. You can
have anything you want to eat.

You can go water skiing, play softball and do anything
you want.

So after all, heaven isn't all that bad.

IT'S GOOD!!!

—Donna

THE METAMORPHOSIS

Characters: The witch
The gorilla
The merry moustached monarch

A long time ago in the day of the dinosaurs, there was a funny little land where people as modern as knights lived. They were ruled by a merry moustached monarch. The monarch used cavemen as slaves. One day he had someone spy around the country to see what he could find. So when the person got back he said that he had seen a witch's castle. A witch's castle? You gotta be crazy! There is no such thing as a witch. There is only as many as there are socks on my feet, and I happen to be barefoot right now. I'll have your name put on the Daily dumb-dumbs list.

The monarch smelled his stinky little feet three times. Pew! Pew! Pew! Out of nowhere the Royal List person came. He bowed low and asked, "Yes, Sire?"

"Put this man's name on the Daily dumb-dumbs list."

The Royal List person wrote it down and disappeared with the man. The monarch was lucky that he didn't have any enemies except dinosaurs because they were stupid. So every time a dinosaur came, the monarch army had to fight it. This day when the monarch was in his throne he saw a dinosaur coming. It was Tyranosaurus. It was one of their most feared dinosaurs. The monarch called on his trumpet and the leader of the army

133

came. The monarch told him to get thirty people of his army to go fight the dinosaur. The leader went out and came back with thirty of his best men. The monarch told them where the dinosaur was and they went off for it. When they found it they rode their horses at top speed at it. They shot arrows at it and they used their spears and lances. Finally the dinosaur rested a while. Then the leader asked which person would be brave enough to climb up his back and dig a hole in his head to kill him. The monarch's son spoke up and armed with his sword, and a pick and shovel to dig with, he started climbing up the dinosaur's back. The dinosaur tried to swish its tail at the Prince, but the Prince kept on dodging it. When he got to the top he just took one pick and the dinosaur went mad. He carried the Prince to the other half of the knightland, which a different king owned. When they went past the other king's palace, the prince jumped off. The dinosaur just kept running. When the Prince got up he saw another Prince, the Prince that lived at that palace. The Prince gave him a horse to get back to the monarch's palace. He rode with him half way, then turned around and went back. When they got back their fathers got made at them and yelled at them. So they had to go to bed hungry. The horse that the Prince had given him was a black stallion, and it was fast as lightning. So after a while Robin Hood declared war on the monarch. The monarch asked the other king for help and they gave it to them. But the two princes were mad at their fathers and hated them so they joined with Robin Hood to march against their fathers. Robin Hood said that he wasn't really born yet but was sent from Heaven to destroy the two kings because they had come too soon. So the princes mounted their horses. Each of them had black stallions. Robin Hood and his men had horses, too. Robin Hood had a bay with a golden tint and his men had black and white ponies, brown, black, or white horses.

So they started riding out. All Robin's men had was bows and arrows, so the princes managed to find some swords for them. Then they rode out. Pretty soon they saw the monarch and king coming. Then they met and charged each other with lances. The two princes were the only ones with armor on Robin Hood's side, and it was pure silver. They charged each other and fought for a while. But Robin Hood was outnumbered and he retreated. But pretty soon he had gotten more men and he marched on again. When they met they started fighting with their swords. They had to use their shields to block the blows. Then both sides held fire. They got their bows and arrows. They sent a line up and shot. In a couple of days the monarch and king went to the monarch's palace. Then Robin Hood attacked with catapults and started to knock the walls of the palace down. The knights were shooting arrows at Robin Hood's men. *Then Robin Hood had the men get in boats and go across the moat and break the drawbridge down, for his palace was more like a castle than a palace. Then they started fighting inside. The monarch and king went to the king's palace. Robin Hood started fighting again and this time since there wasn't a moat around this palace they broke the door down and rode up the steps into the palace and fought on horses. Then they killed all of the people and took all the riches up to Heaven. The princes went too, taking a princess. That night a dinosaur said, "It sure is nice now that the monarch and king are gone. And that guy was stupid, thinking he saw a witch! He was stupid."*

"What did you say, pokey?" said a witch flying by. "Well, take that," she said. ZOP! She turned him into a little green man and flew away on her broom.

—Gilbert Varney

METAMORPHOSIS

I went down to Gray's auction the other night. There were a lot of people there and they were buying a lot of stuff. I bought a Billy Goat for eighteen dollars.

The Goat's name was Mac. He had strange yellow eyes. I made the mistake of staring into his eyes. The next thing I knew the only thing I could say was "baa, baa, baa."

The next thing I knew my ears were starting to grow hair on them. Then I started growing a tail. Then my face started to change into a Billy Goat's.

Mr Gray took one look at me and started to auction me off. So I dug my hooves into the ground, (I had hooves by now, you see) put my head down, and bucked him in the rear.

Then Mac, the other Billy Goat, came along and thought that I was his father. All the people stood up and started yelling because they were afraid of me and Mac. I was embarrassed.

I decided to get in my car and drive home so no one could see me. But the moment I got out on the highway, the State Highway Patrolman passed by. He took one look at me, his mouth fell open with surprise, and started chasing me.

135

Mac was riding in the car with me. To my surprise, I learned that Mac had my voice now. He could talk. Mac told me to pull over.

I pulled over. The Highway Patrolman got out of his car and came over to us. Then Mac asked him what was the matter. The policeman said, "I have never seen a Billy Goat driving a car, and I have never seen a talking Billy Goat." I got out of the car and bucked him one right in the gut. Then we went home and had tin cans for supper. Then we went to bed.

In the morning the TV repairman came. I was too tired to get up so Mac answered the door. "Come on in," said Mac. (Mac was always quite friendly, you see.) The TV repairman turned pale, he got a glazed look in his eyes, then he fell over, flat on his back.

Mac came in and woke me up. "The TV repairman has fallen down in our front yard," Mac said. "We've got to get him out of here before the neighbors get suspicious."

So we went upstairs and got a stretcher and put him back in his car. After one hour he woke up and came to the door again. This time I answered the door so the TV repairman wouldn't turn pale and faint. It didn't work. He fainted again.

Mac came downstairs, took one look and said, "We've really got to get him out of here now. The neighbors will think we've murdered someone. Then they'll come and take me back to Gray's auction. Oh, don't let them take me back there, it's awful."

We decided to throw the TV repairman into the trunk and take him to another town. We forgot that my gossipy neighbor, Mrs. Sniggles, was watching us from her window the whole time.

After we left, Mrs. Sniggles called the police. The police came and investigated around our house and in our house. By this time we were in another town. We stopped at a store to get something to drink. Mrs. Sniggles had given them a description of our car. We were in the store when all of a sudden we heard the police.

136

They saw our car and started to come in when we found a
back door and Mac got his foot caught. The police saw
Mac's tail and went to the back door. Just as one policeman
opened the door and was ready to grab Mac, Mac let his foot
fly and hit the policeman right in the mouth and knocked
him over backwards.

I was waiting for Mac in the car when Mac came running out
and almost tripped over a rock. As soon as Mac was in, I
hit the gas peddle and went down the street. Mac looked
out the back window and saw the police right behind us.

Ahead of us was a big barn so I told Mac to get ready
for a good ride. I told Mac we would go right through
the barn. But just as we got to it I saw that the door
was closed. I was going too fast to stop and open the
door, so I just went right on through the door.

When we came out the police were still behind us. It
was hard to see because there was hay all over the car.
There was a chicken in the back seat and a pig on the roof.

We were going about ninety miles an hour when all of a sudden
the pig fell through the roof. Mac and I tried to put it
in the back seat. Mac and I were paying so much attention
to the pig that we didn't see the police coming for us.

Then Mac looked up and saw the police car and told me.
I turned off the road and went through a brook. There
was so much sand and leaves that I couldn't see out the
window. I was going back and forth through the trees
when there was a big crash and a big jerk. Mac and I got
out. The car was all smashed up.

Mac and I started running. We were running so fast that
we forgot all about the TV repairman who was in the trunk.
We kept on running until we came to a town where there were
a lot of stores, banks, hotels and gas stations. So we went
into a gas station and back out, and then we went up to the
top floor of a hotel and then started back down the fire
escape.

I looked over at Mac. He was smiling. He seemed to be enjoying
himself. "Ya know what, my friend," Mac said, "I think I'm
really a mountain goat. I just love it up here." I looked
down. We were about twenty stories high, and the people

137

*below looked just like little ants and their cars looked
like toy cars.*

*I still wasn't used to having hooves instead of feet. I
could feel myself slipping. It was hard to hold on. Mac
said, "Wow, this is great! The air up here is fantastic!
Let's go up higher." And before I could motion to Mac to
tell him to hang on to me, he was going up, up, up.*

*When we got up the next floor I slipped and really
fell. I was trying to make my tail into a propeller, but
I was going too fast. I was twirling and spinning. Mac
was still going up and up. I was still falling when Mac
turned around and saw me.*

*I fell right into the seat of a traffic helicopter and
knocked the announcer and the driver out. So I started
driving it up and dropped a hook to Mac to pick him up
and put him in the helicopter beside me.*

*We were flying over Elm Street when we heard the traffic
radio. So Mac picked it up and said "This is traffic
helicopter 43691 reporting. The traffic is terrible on
Elm Street. Sick Street is clear. There aren't any cars
along Sick Street."*

*I think Mac was a little mixed up because I looked down
and saw that Sick Street was already full of cars. And more
and more cars were turning onto Sick Street every minute
because of Mac's announcement. Then I saw one car coming
around the corner being chased by a police car, just as
a big trailer truck was coming the other way and plowed
right into the police car.*

*The policeman got out and put handcuffs on the truckdriver.
The street was getting more and more crowded every minute.
People started leaning on their horns. It was bumper to
bumper. Some guy got out of his car and called the policeman
a jerk and punched him on the nose. Three or four people
came to help the policeman. Other people came to help the
truck driver.*

*Soon everybody was fighting. A towtruck came along to
pick up the police car and plowed into a whole line of
cars. It hit one car so hard the car bumped into a fire*

hydrant and the fire hydrant exploded. Two or three cars burst into flame.

Mac looked down Sick Street and started laughing. Then he looked over at Elm Street—it was empty. All of a sudden the helicopter started coughing. Mac was scared. He started fooling around with the controls, but it got worse and worse. Then I looked down at the gas gauge. It was right on empty. We started falling. All of a sudden there was a big bang and we came to a sudden stop. We had landed right on top of the city jail.

They put us in a dingy, dark, sickening, awful cell. Then the police left. Mac started to cry, and great big tears ran down his whiskers.

It was about a week before anyone came with any food. Mac was talking to me when a guard came walking by and fainted right in front of the cell. Mac stuck his horns out through the bars and got the keys off his belt. Then Mac opened the door.

We ran down the hallway. We looked out a window and saw two policemen coming. So Mac and I found some police jackets and hid behind them. The police came in and walked right by us. Then Mac and I ran to the front door and went out.

We were running down the street when an ambulance came down the street. Mac looked at it as it went by and said, "It's the TV repairman. They found him." Now Mac was really scared.

Just then five men got out of a car and surrounded us. They stood there for a minute and then one of them said, "Put them in the car and take them to the courthouse." Another one said, "Put them in a cell until their trial."

They took us into the courthouse and brought us to a cell in the back of the courtroom. Mac was crying. He said, "Now we're doomed!"

Our trial started three weeks later. The courtroom was filled with people. Mac and I walked in, with our heads bent down, feeling terrible. We looked at the crowd. Suddenly, a woman screamed, "Oh, oh, there they are, there they are." It was Mrs. Sniggles. "Oh dear, oh, those nasty, dirty goats. I saw them hit that poor TV repairman on the head and throw him into the trunk of a car."

Then we saw the TV repairman. One of his legs and one of his arms was in a cast, and there was a great big bandage on his head. Some of his teeth had been knocked out, too. He jumped up and pointed at us and tried to say "That's them," but he could only mumble "Mat's mem" through all those bandages.

Then a policeman came over and took us to where we were supposed to sit. There were a lot of people there. They were all yelling and screaming at us. The helicopter driver and the announcer were there with a broken jaw and a broken arm. The man at the gas station was there. The pig and the chicken were even there. The pig had some scrapes and bruises on his stomach from when he fell through the roof. The policeman and the truck driver who had the fight on Sick Street were there, too.

Finally, the judge came in and shouted, "Order in the court." But nobody came to order. The TV repairman kept jumping up and down and shouting "mat's mem! mat's mem! mat's mem!" And old Mrs. Sniggles kept yelling, "Oh, oh my, oh dear, those dirty, nasty, horrible goats!"

"We're done for," Mac said. "These people really hate us."

And Mac was right. A moment later somebody in the crowd threw a brick at us, and they just missed. Then another brick was thrown. This one hit me on top of my head. It almost broke one of my horns.

I reached up to see if I was bleeding when I noticed—the hair on my ears was disappearing. Then all the hair on me started to go away. I realized that I didn't have any clothes on, and I ran over and grabbed the judge's robe and wrapped it around me. Then my feet began to change back and my hands began to change back. I wiggled my toes for the first time in a month. It felt wonderful.

The people were flabbergasted. They put down their bricks and they stopped shouting and they just stared at us. I looked over at Mac and whispered, "Mac, I'm changing." But Mac couldn't answer. He just sat there, trying to say something, and I think he looked a little sad.

The Judge said, "Case dismissed." His hands were trembling, and he reached quickly into his drawer for some pills.

I put Mac on a leash, and we walked out of the courtroom and went home. We were free.

THE END

—Larry Farnham & Dick Murphy

MY SHADOW

On a foggy day in the winter my shadow hides from me,
and in a storm it seems like it's gone forever.
One day I followed my shadow when it was storming.
It went up into the dark blue sky.
I couldn't fly up in the sky after it,
so I climbed up a mountain.
It beat me up there
but I could still see where it was going.
A bald eagle started to dive at me and
my shadow was frightened.
It went up to the bald eagle's nest
to hide in it.
The bald eagle wanted to protect her babies
and found my shadow there.
My shadow started to run to me
the eagle was right on its tail
Then I started to throw rocks at the eagle,
then I threw them at her nest.
She had to go back to her nest so
her eggs wouldn't crack and her babies wouldn't die.
My shadow and I went home.
My shadow said he was never going to
hide in a storm again.

—Debby Chapin

HALFTE DES LEBENS

Mit gelben Birnen hanget
Und voll mit wilden Rosen
Das Land in Den See,
Ihr holden Schwane,
Und Trunken von Kussen
Trunkt ihr das Haupt
Ins heilignuchterne Wasser.

Weh mir, wo nehm ich, wenn
Es Winter ist, die Blumen, und wo
Den Sonnenschein
Und Schatten der Erde?
Die Mauern stehn
Sprachlos und kalt, im Winde
Klirren die Fahnen.

(Original German, by Holderlin)

When Glenden hung Bernie
those with wild roses
Died in the land of Den See.
Then when Holden Schwane
Told me not to see Bernie
He saw the beer and got drunk.

Cindy Claflin

When golden Birch and hanging,
And rich with wild rose,
The land in Springtime
Hold Mysteries
To those who kiss,
Tramping through the hills
In spectacular color.

Who me, to kiss, you're fooling.
To win her yes. She's beautiful
In summertime,
In Statenburg we will
Get married.
Springtime, fall, and Winter,
Kissing by the Fire.

Regina Rafferty

The Golden Birds of the Hamlet
Ate the wild roses
Of the Land and the Sea.
The Holy King of Trunken
Sent Sir Kussen on a trip.
He was to go to Wasser Island
To kill the Golden Birds.
As winter first set in,
He was dead
A blueman blue.

Michael Fletcher

HALF THE TIME

Mister Gwen Ben burned himself
When he got hanged and vomited
On a bunch of wild roses,
Given to him by
The Land of Den Dee.
When he was holding the Swan
His mother had given him
A trunk fell on him,
And it happened that he died.

He had an itch, when he was in
His grave. Then, when he scratched it,
Winter came. The people that came
To his funeral sang
A sonnet
Of the snow.

Jimmy Flanders

My golden brown hair
Is filled with wild roses
On the bottom of the sea.
I hold my lover
In my short arms
I stare him in the eye
And kiss him on the cheek.

He asks me
To marry him.
I said I would
But I may be wrong.
It will be a blessing
If I do.

Donna Cramer

My green bloomers are hanging
Under the wilting roses.
From land and sea
Golden swans
And drunken fishers
Pack their trunks
To come and see my bloomers.

Why me? Who named Me?
When winter comes my roses die.
My bloomers fall.
The summer comes
And my green bloomers
Come back.

Maura Rafferty

(Real Translation)

The Middle of Life

With yellow pears and full of wild
roses the land hangs down into
the lakes, you lovely swans, and
drunken with kisses you dip your
head into the holy and sober
water.

Alas, where shall I find, when
winter comes, the flowers, and
where the sunshine and shadows
of earth? The walls loom
speechless and cold, in the wind
weathercocks clatter.

144

*** *** COMING TO FAIRLEE *** ***

THE
    FLOATING
        LOG

WITH: *—Mr. Dingberry imitating apples falling off an apple tree.*

(and)   *—The Fascinating "Go-Go" the Monkey with his magnificent music box.*

This show will be delayed in case of a flood.

DON'T MISS: *—Three (3) purple frogs and an E*Y*E*B*L*U*S*H-I*N*G Kawisaki race. Come see the race at 3:00. They will be running the full length of the log—two feet.*

THIS IS THE BEST SHOW ON EARTH!!!!!
Bring your bawlbabies and your older kids.

COME: *—See the singing contest and crack your ears!*

DANCE: *—With the polka dotted polka, or, if you would rather, you can dance to one.*

SEE: *—the BLIND DINGBAT named Edith.*

THIS SHOW WILL REALLY LIGHT YOUR EYES UP
LIKE A FORTY WATT LIGHT BULB!!!

(for fat ladies only)

Come AND TRY our ALL NEW stomach S*H*R*I*N*K*E*R
SEE the WALKING Encyclopedia

You will love our show — It is WONDERFUL & AMUSING

See 18 (eighteen) marbles r - o - l - l

                                    p
                                u

                        A HILL

***Buy the only glue that WON'T stick.

***See the only witness to the ROBBERY at Mac's Creek
—the eyewitness is A PETUNIA.

***See the greatest thing on earth—a DUMMY that's a
REAL PERSON.

***See the Three Blind Mice singing "How Fast Do Turtles
Go" and cracking eggs, not jokes.

(Your family will L O V E THIS SHOW)

COME — PLAY — OUR — GAMES
They are SPIN THE VITAMIN BOTTLE
(that game is for babies, only)

COME — SEE — THE — SKINNIEST — Σ*L*E*P*H*A*N*T
(named Snake)

If you want you can get squished by a Kangaroo
AND BECOME A PAPER DOLL

***See the only Crisp Cereal that Really Flies
***See MERLIN THE MAGICIAN Shrink a Head
***SEE the Roncasoris Polo Game

THIS IS SOMETHING YOU WON'T SEE
—pebbles and BAM BAM hit you on the head

★ ★

LOOK at the psychodelic FAT LADY'S underwear
GO
SEE
BENNIE'S FASHIONS
HE
HAS
SOME

Holy Underwear & he has some psychodelic underwear
like the fat ladies.

COME *** RIDE THE BIGGEST ROLLER COASTER
SEE *** THE FIRST RUBBER BABY BUMPER IN THE WORLD

SEE
the
book
worm

do
his
squiggle
dance

And —YOU— can see Mr. Dingberry —AGAIN—
doing his imitation of DREAM WHIP
coming out of the SQUEEZE CONTAINER

DROP
IN AND WATCH OUR DROP
IN MOVIES HIT PEOPLE
ON THE HEAD.

Look at the WHIRLING SUPER ©))''#5•$__&©'__)&'©__
500 (Five Hundred) HURRICANE

Your eyes won't believe what you'll see on the floating log. It will be roll-
ing down the Connecticut River at around three o'clock. It will be in
Fairlee ·FOR AS LONG AS IT TAKES THE MOTOR TO GO. The
Floating Log is sponsored by the Lake Morey Inn. THANK YOU.
THANK YOU. THANK YOU. THANK YOU. THANK YOU. THANK

WHO KNOWS
(a play with music)
by Darren Vietje

TIME: The Gold Rush, 1858.   *PLACE: Hangman's Gulch*
CHARACTERS: Bucktooth Bill
Hurricane Hank   *Prospectors*
Tiger Lily: The beautiful owner of the Golden Spike
Saloon
Slimy Sam Stretchneck: The villain

147

(Main Street, Hangman's Gulch. The Golden Spike Saloon is in the back of the stage. Bucktooth and Hurricane walk into town. They are wearing rotten old clothes. Bucktooth carries a pick and Hurricane carries a shovel.)

Bucktooth:	Been five days without food or drink.
Hurricane:	Yup.
Bucktooth:	Only got a little money, a pick and a shovel, and the clothes on our backs. We gotta strike it rich here and now, or we're through, Hurricane.
Hurricane:	Yup.
Bucktooth:	This here town's called Hangman's Gulch. 'Spozed to be a real tough town.
Hurricane:	Yup.
Bucktooth:	But, who knows, maybe our luck will change here.
Hurricane:	Yup.
Bucktooth:	Can't you say anything but "yup?"
Hurricane:	Yup.
Bucktooth:	Well, what else can you say then?
Hurricane:	Let's go in and have a drink at the Golden Spike Saloon.
Bucktooth:	For once I agree with ya. We've been five days without food or drink. Let's go in.

(They walk slowly into the bar. It is empty except for Tiger Lily. She is a beautiful blonde. Both men stare at her throughout the scene. They can't keep their eyes off her.)

Tiger Lily:	Hi, boys, what can I do for you?

(Their mouths fall open. For a moment they cannot speak.)

Tiger Lily:	Well now, boys, what'll it be?
Hurricane:	Uhhh, ummm, I'll have ahh bah, bah, bah beer. I mean bear. I mean beer. I'll have a beer.
Bucktooth:	Wha, wha, wha whiskey. Whiskey for me, please, miss.

(Tiger Lily disappears behind the bar to get the drinks.)

Hurricane:	Did you see what I saw?
Bucktooth:	Did I see what you saw?
Hurricane:	Did I see what you saw?
Bucktooth:	Did I see what you saw?

Hurricane:	*Shhhhhhhhh.*
Bucktooth:	*Shhhhhhhhh.*
Tiger Lily:	*Here you are, boys. One beer. One whiskey.*

(They gulp it down)

Say, where are you boys from?

(Hurricane and Bucktooth sing "The Songs of the Blue Mountain Boys")

Tiger Lily: *My, my, my, my. I didn't know you boys were singers.*

Bucktooth: *We're not. We're plumbers.*

Hurricane: *Ha! Ha! He, he, he! Ha! Ha! He, he, he!*

Bucktooth: *Ha! Ha! That was just a joke. We really are prospectors, down on our luck. And what is your name, if you don't mind my askin', Miss?*

Tiger Lily: *I'm called Tiger Lily around these parts.*

Hurricane: *Mighty pleased to meet you, Tiger Lily.*

Bucktooth: *Tiger Lily. That sure is a purty name. Just like a flower.*

Hurricane: *An awful purty flower.*

Tiger Lily: *Now, now boys. (Changing the subject) How about one on the house?*

Hurricane: *One what?*

Bucktooth: *Shut up, you. Don't mind him, Tiger Lily. He fell off his horse when he was only six. It's touched him a little. Sure, I'd like another whiskey.*

Hurricane: *And I'll have a beer.*

Tiger Lily: *So, you boys have come to Hangman's Gulch to strike it rich.*

Bucktooth: *That's about the size of it, Miss.*

Tiger Lily: *Well, a lot of men have come to Hangman's Gulch for gold, but they've all ended up on Boot Hill. Take a look out the window there. See those grave markers? A lot of men are layin' there. Some 'cause they was good, some 'cause they was bad, and all 'cause they were dead, by George.*

(Hurricane and Bucktooth look out the window)

Bucktooth: *Well, Tiger Lily, like I said, we're down on our luck. We*

149

	can't move on. We gotta strike it rich here and now, or we're through.
Hurricane:	Yup.
Tiger Lily:	Well, good luck, boys.
Bucktooth:	It's too bad we have to sleep out in the rain, on the cold, wet ground.
Tiger Lily:	There might be an empty room I could let you have upstairs. Cheap.
Bucktooth:	What are your dates? I mean rates.
Tiger Lily:	Oh, we don't bill you until the next day.
Bucktooth:	Any bill is more than we can afford to pay right now. I guess we'll have to sleep out in the rain again tonight.
Hurricane:	Yup.
Tiger Lily:	Well, OK, so long boys.
Bucktooth:	Just a minute. Could you take a rain check, Miss?
Hurricane:	Ha! Ha! He, he, he. Ha! Ha! He, he, he!
Tiger Lily:	I said, so long, boys. It's past closing time.
	(Bucktooth & Hurricane don't really want to leave)
Hurricane:	So long, Tiger Lily.
Bucktooth:	So long, Tiger Lily.

(They back away from her, still not able to take their eyes off her. At the doorway, they stumble into each other. The curtain goes down)

SCENE II

(That night, Tiger Lily's bedroom window. The window is closed. The stage is empty. Suddenly somebody comes sneaking quietly on stage. It is Bucktooth Bill. He looks cautiously over his shoulder, knocks over a garbage can, picks it up quickly, falls. Waits. Scared somebody might have heard him. But it is quiet. Finally, he taps on Tiger Lily's window.)

Bucktooth:	Tiger Lily, wake up. Please wake up. I must talk to you. Just talk to me for a minute. We met today. It's me, Bucktooth Bill. Please come to your window.
Tiger Lily:	What's going on? It's late, it's late, it's late.
Bucktooth:	But it's a very important date.

150

Tiger Lily:	*(Opens the window, looks down and sees Bucktooth Bill)* Oh, it's you. What do you want?
Bucktooth:	*(SINGS THE "Love Duet")* Ah, shucks, Tiger Lily. Please marry me.
Tiger Lily:	Well, Bucktooth. You are kinda cute. And I do like you. I'll tell you what, if you ever do strike it rich, of course I'll marry you. Just bring me back a million or two and I'll be your blushing bride.
Bucktooth:	*(Really excited)* Do you really mean it, Tiger Lily? You really will marry me?
Tiger Lily:	Sure I mean it, Bucktooth.
Bucktooth:	Well golly gee, goobers in a hat. Tiger Lily, I'll be seein' ya.
Tiger Lily:	Yea. I'll be seein' ya. *(Whispers)* Clutza.

(He leaves. She closes the window)

(For a while the stage is empty. Suddenly someone comes sneaking across the stage. It is Hurricane Hank. He looks cautiously over his shoulder, trips over the garbage can, etc. Finally he taps on Tiger Lily's window)

Hurricane:	Tiger Lily! Tiger Lily! Wake up! Wake up! I must talk to you. It's me, Hurricane Hank. Please come to your window.
Tiger Lily:	Oh, no! Not again. I haven't gotten a wink of sleep all night. *(She opens the window)* Ok, ok, hold your horses. What is it this time?
Hurricane:	Tiger Lily. Oh, Tiger Lily. From the moment I first saw you at the Golden Spike Saloon, I knew you were for me, honey. Your golden hair, your wonderful complexion, your deep blue eyes, your little button nose, your....
Tiger Lily:	Ok, ok. Look, I've got neighbors who think I'm a respectable woman. Now, if you want to marry me, just say so and get it over with.
Hurricane:	*(He sings the same "Love Duet")* Ah, shucks, Tiger Lily. Please marry me.
Tiger Lily:	Well, Hurricane, you are kinda cute. And I do like you. I'll tell you what. If you ever strike it rich, of course I'll marry ya. Just bring me back a million or two and I'll be your blushin' bride forever.

151

Hurricane:	(Excited) Do ya really mean it, Tiger Lily? You really will marry me?
Tiger Lily:	Sure I mean it, Hurricane.
Hurricane:	Well, golly gee. Goobers in a hat. I'll be seein' ya, Tiger Lily.
Tiger Lily:	Yea. See ya around. (Whispers) Clutza.

(Curtain)

SCENE III

(It is the next morning at the Golden Spike Saloon)

(Slimy Sam Stretchneck is standing at the bar, very cool and looking smart, twirling his moustache. He takes five or six drinks, but they don't affect him a bit. He is just as cool as ever)

Slimy Sam:	(Calling to the back of the bar) Hey there, beautiful. Could ya get me another bottle?
Tiger Lily:	(Entering) Good morning, Slimy. How ya doin' today?
Slimy Sam:	Oh, things are a little slow today, baby. Seems like I've already swindled most everyone out of their money. I sure wish some new folks would come to town.
Tiger Lily:	Yea. I know what you mean. This is a real hick town. Hardly anything exciting happens here.
Slimy Sam:	Well, I'm here, baby, and I'm excitin'.
Tiger Lily:	Yea, but you're different, Slimy. Say, that reminds me. I met a couple of real clutzes last night. I don't know if they have any money, but if they do, it would be for the takin'.
Slimy Sam:	Sounds good, baby. Where are they?

(Hurricane and Bucktooth come in)

(Tiger Lily makes herself look busy. Slimy Sam approaches Bucktooth and Hurricane)

Slimy Sam:	Hi ya boys. Welcome to Hangman's Gulch. I hear tell you boys are prospectors. Want to strike it rich.
Hurricane:	Yup.
Slimy Sam:	Well, let me tell you about a once-in-a-lifetime deal.
Bucktooth:	(Interested) Sure, tell us.
Slimy Sam:	Then listen very carefully to this.

(Slimy Sam sings the song of the "Land Deal")

152

(All the time Slimy Sam is singing, Tiger Lily laughs to herself behind the bar. She laughs so hard she even chokes on her drink)

Tiger Lily: That's Slimy Sam Stretchneck for you. He never lies. Never.

Slimy Sam: Never.

Bucktooth: That sure sounds interestin'. That sounds like what we've been lookin' for, doesn't it, Hurricane?

Hurricane: Yup.

Bucktooth: How can you prove this is a real deal?

(Very quickly Tiger Lily starts writing behind the bar so that Hurricane and Bucktooth can't see)

Slimy Sam: *(Trying to stall for time)* Well, number one. This is a real deal because you're dealing with Slimy Sam Stretchneck. Number two, I never lie.

Tiger Lily: Never. *(She secretly hands him the writing)*

Slimy Sam: And, number three, I happen to have the deed to the property right here in my hand.

Hurricane: A deed! Man, that's pretty fancy. I've never seen a real one before. Look here, Bucktooth. Do you see what I see?

Bucktooth: Do I see what you see?

Hurricane: Did he see what I saw?

Bucktooth: Did I see what he saw?

Tiger Lily: Well, boys, here it is. This is your chance to strike it rich. *(Sweetly)* And you know what that means.

Bucktooth: That's right. Hey, Hurricane. How much money do you have?

Hurricane: That is right. Hey, Bucktooth, how much money do you have?

Bucktooth: *(Searching his pockets)* We.., I've got one...two...seven ...twelve...four...ah...ummm...Oh, here, Tiger Lily. Here's all my money. You count it.

Tiger Lily: Sure, I'll count it, Bucktooth. *(SHE COUNTS)*

Hurricane: I've got at least two dollars here. Ummm...ahh...um... Here, Tiger Lily, you count my money, too.

Tiger Lily: Sure, I'll count it, Hurricane. *(SHE COUNTS)* Well, boys, you have a grand total of three dollars and 92 cents.

Slimy Sam:	*Well, boys, I guess we'll have to call off the deal. You're three cents short.*
Hurricane & Bucktooth:	*Awwwwwwwwwwww!*
Slimy:	*Well, that's ok. You know me. Mr. Perfect Citizen, Mr. Nice Guy. Since we have such a special friendship, and we never lie, and since I want to help you get your start right here in this friendly little hick town—you just couldn't pick a better place—I'll knock three cents off the original price.*
Bucktooth:	*You will! You'll really knock three live American cents off the original price!*
Slimy Sam:	*I sure will.*
Tiger Lily:	*He sure will.*
Slimy Sam:	*The land is yours.*
Hurricane & Bucktooth:	*Wow! Gee! Wow! Gee!*
Tiger Lily:	*Well, boys, what do ya say? Aren't you forgetting to thank Slimy Sam?*
Hurricane:	*Thank you, Slimy.*
Bucktooth:	*Thank you, Slimy.*

(Curtain)

SCENE IV

(Three months have gone by. Hurricane and Bucktooth are crawling on the ground dragging their picks and shovels behind them)

Bucktooth:	*Nope. Not yet.*
Hurricane:	*Yup.*
Bucktooth:	*Nope, Not yet.*
Hurricane:	*Yup.*
Bucktooth:	*Nope, not yet.*
Hurricane:	*Yup.*
Bucktooth:	*Nope, not yet.*
Hurricane:	*Yup.*
Bucktooth:	*Nope, not yet.*
Hurricane:	*Yup.*

Bucktooth:	*Hey, Hurricane. I'm beginning to get mad. I am beginning to think that deal we made with Slimy Sam Stretchneck was a little off balance (if you know what I mean).*
Hurricane:	*Yup. I know what you mean.*
Bucktooth:	*We've been here for three months, Hurricane. I'm beginning to get hungry.*
Hurricane:	*Yup. Been three months without food or drink.*
Bucktooth:	*And thirsty.*
Hurricane:	*Three months without food or drink.*
Bucktooth:	*You know, Hurricane, I'm beginning to think that Stretchneck guy is a low-down creep, if you know what I mean.*
Hurricane:	*Yup. A low-down creep.*
Bucktooth:	*Can't hold on much longer. Sure don't look like there's any gold here.*
Hurricane:	*Yup. No gold here.*
Bucktooth:	*And where's that shack he told us about?*
Hurricane:	*Yup. Ain't no shack.*
Bucktooth:	*And what about that stream? And them fish?*
Hurricane:	*Yup. Ain't no stream! Ain't no fish!*
Bucktooth:	*This land don't supply my every wish. Right?*
Hurricane:	*Right. Sorry. I mean yup.*
Bucktooth:	*I'd like to punch that Stretchneck one in the nose.*
Hurricane:	*Yup. In the nose.*
Bucktooth:	*(Looking down) See that rock down there? Doesn't that remind you of something?*
Hurricane:	*Yup. That reminds me of a rock.*
Bucktooth:	*Well, it reminds me of that Stretchneck. (To the rock) Slimy Sam, take that! (He slams his pick into the rock) Womp!*
Hurricane:	*(Watching) Yup. Womp!*

(Both of them look closely at the rock. Their mouths fall open. Slowly, Bucktooth reaches into the hole he has made in the rock. He pulls out a beer bottle. Then he reaches in again and pulls out a huge gold rock)

Bucktooth:	*Gold!*
Hurricane:	*Gold!*
Bucktooth:	*Gold!*

Hurricane:	*Gold!*
Bucktooth:	*Gold!*
Hurricane:	*Gold!*
Bucktooth:	*Gold!*
Hurricane:	*Gold!*
Bucktooth:	*Gold!*
Hurricane:	*Yup. Gold.*

(They sing the "Song of Being Rich")

(Curtain)

SCENE V

(A few days later. Back at the Golden Spike Saloon. Tiger Lily is working behind the bar as usual. Slimy Sam is drinking at the bar as usual)

Slimy Sam: Hey, beautiful, could ya get me another bottle?

Tiger Lily: Sure, Slimy. You sure know how to hold your whiskey.

Slimy Sam: You bet, baby. Hey, are you busy tonight? I was thinking of having a little party.

Tiger Lily: I'm never too busy for Stretchneck. Besides, things are a little slow. I wish some more strangers would come to town, liven things up a bit. Like those two suckers that came in a few months ago. Remember those clutzas? I wonder whatever happened to them.

Slimy Sam: Ah, what difference does it make? We got their money, baby, that's all that counts. Anyways, I've sold that same piece of land two hundred times, and nobody ever came back yet. I sure would have liked to have see'd their faces when they were out there dyin' of thirst. Ha. Ha. Ha.

Tiger Lily: Slimy, you really are smart.

Slimy Sam: I know it, baby. I know it.

(Hurricane and Bucktooth enter. They are all cleaned up and they are wearing suits and ties. Since they are not used to wearing good clothes, they should look a little funny, like their suits don't really fit. They are carrying a big piece of gold)

Slimy Sam: (Not noticing them) I am smart, baby. I sure would have liked to have see'd their faces when they were out there dyin' of thirst. I never met two such stupid clutzas.

156

Tiger Lily:	*(Beginning to wonder) (Looking at the gold)* Yeh, you're smart, all right.
Slimy Sam:	*(Still not noticing them)* Yeh. I am smart.
Bucktooth:	Gold!
Hurricane:	Gold!
Bucktooth:	Gold!
Hurricane:	Yup. Gold.
Slimy Sam:	*(Seeing them and the gold for the first time)* What? You mean you clutzas found gold on that worthless, good for nothing, dried up, rotten old sandbar that I tricked you into buying? I mean that I, I . . .
Hurricane:	Yup. Gold.
Tiger Lily:	Say, Slimy, maybe I am just a little bit busy tonight. How 'bout a couple of drinks, boys. On the house. We have a new deal here—as many as you can hold, for just a piece of gold. So you're so smart, eh Slimy?—Here ya are, Bucktooth. On the house. Real smart, huh, Slimy?—Here ya are, Hurricane.
Slimy Sam:	Now listen here, boys. You're new around here. You don't seem to understand our local law and policies. For example *(He pulls out a town report)* according to our town report —law "A", on page 43, section 'B', paragraph 18 on land ownership says, and I quote, "Whereas all prospectors shall furnish proof positive of rightful ownership of land wherefrom which gold was found." In other words, boys, that's my gold.
Bucktooth & Hurricane:	Who? What? Where? When? Why and how and sometimes whom?
Bucktooth:	But we have the deed right here. Signed by Slimy Sam Stretchneck himself.
Tiger Lily:	I'm afraid they've got ya this time, Slimy. You'll just have to swallow hard and take it.
Slimy Sam:	All right. Alright. I'm going. But listen here, you two bananas. You haven't heard even the beginning of this.
Bucktooth:	Sure, we heard the beginning. We were both acting in the first scene.
Hurricane:	Yup. First scene.

157

Slimy Sam:	*No. No. I don't mean that beginning. I mean a new beginning, you morons. Now listen to Slimy. You might have been smart enough to find gold, but ya sure ain't smart enough to keep it.*
Tiger Lily:	*Oh, leave them alone, Slimy.*

(Slimy goes stomping out)

Tiger Lily:	*Well, boys, I guess I sort of misjudged ya. I've seen hundreds of men buy that same old piece of worthless land. But you are the only two that ever came back.*
Bucktooth:	*That's cause it really takes brains to find gold, Tiger Lily.*
Hurricane:	*Yup, brains.*
Tiger Lily:	*Well, now that you've got all this gold, how much can your pockets hold? In other words, what are you going to do with all that money?*
Bucktooth:	*Ah, shucks, Tiger Lily, you know.*
Hurricane:	*Yeh. Shucks, Tiger Lily, you know.*
Bucktooth:	*You remember what you said, don't ya, Tiger Lily?*
Hurricane:	*Yea. You remember what you said, don't ya, Tiger Lily?*
Bucktooth:	*'Bout what happens when I strike it rich.*
Hurricane:	*'Bout what happens when I strike it rich.*
Bucktooth:	*Hey, Hurricane, have you forgotten your lines again? You not s'pozed to be talkin' to her in this scene. She said she'd be my blushin' bride.*
Hurricane:	*You're mixed up. Hey, Prompter! Tell Bucktooth he's messin' up this play. She's s'pozed to be my blushin' bride.*
iger Lily:	*Blushin' bride. Who says I've got anything to blush about?*
Bucktooth:	*Hurricane, she said she'd marry me in the song.*
Hurricane:	*No Bucktooth, she said she'd marry me in the song.*
Bucktooth:	*Was you sung the same song that I was sung?*
Hurricane:	*Was I sung the same song that he was sung?*
Bucktooth:	*Was he sung the same song that I was sung?*
Hurricane:	*Was he sung the same song that I was sung?*
Tiger Lily:	*(Quickly stepping in. Handingout the dueling guns.) Take your pick, boys. You ain't got no other choice. Since you're both in love with me, I guess you'll have to fight over me.*

158

Bucktooth:	Well, Hurricane, I guess she's right. It's got to be one or the other of us.
Hurricane:	Yup. One or the other.
Bucktooth:	It's too bad it's got to end this way, Hurricane. Twenty-five years of friendship down the drain.
Hurricane:	Yup. Down the drain.
Bucktooth:	Ya sure you wouldn't rather go away and just leave her to me? Then at least we could both stay alive.
Hurricane:	Nope. But you could go away and leave her to me.
Bucktooth:	Nope.
Hurricane:	Nope.
Bucktooth:	Well, I guess this is how it's going to have to end.
Hurricane:	Yup.
Bucktooth:	I'll be seein' ya, Hurricane. May we meet again someday, way up in them clouds that is the last restin' place for lonesome prospectors like you and me.
Hurricane:	Yup. I'll be seein' ya, Bucktooth. Someday. Somehow. Somewhere.
Tiger Lily:	Come on, let's get on with it. Ain't got all day.
Hurricane:	(Almost crying) Goodbye, Bucktooth.
Bucktooth:	(Also nearly in tears) So long, Hurricane.
Hurricane:	I'll try not to hurt ya much.
Bucktooth:	And I'll try not to hurt you.

(Drums start to roll, they take 10 steps, turn around and face each other. Then stand staring at each other)

Tiger Lily:	Draw.

(Instead of drawing, Hurricane and Bucktooth drop their guns, run together and hug each other)

Bucktooth:	I can't do it Hurricane.
Hurricane:	I can't do it, Bucktooth.
Tiger Lily:	Oh, sure ya can, boys.

(They both look at Tiger Lily, the drums start to roll again. They pace off their steps)

Tiger Lily:	Draw.

(This time Hurricane and Bucktooth take magic markers from their pockets and start drawing pictures of stick men on the walls)

159

Tiger Lily: Once more, boys, I know you're a little slow getting the hang of it, but let's give it one more try.

(They look at Tiger Lily again. The drums start to roll, they pace off their steps)

Tiger Lily: Draw.

(This time they shoot. Lots of shots. Slowly they both sink down to their knees. Together Hurricane and Bucktooth sing the slow version of the "Blue Mountain Boys" as they die. Then they kick the bucket)

Tiger Lily: *(Picking up the gold rock and hiding it behind the bar as Slimy Sam comes back in)* Hi ya, Slimy.

Slimy Sam: *(Stepping over the bodies)* Good work, baby.

Tiger Lily: Can I get you a drink, Slimy. We have a new deal. "As much as you can hold, for just a piece of gold."

Slimy Sam: Don't mind if I do.

Tiger Lily: How's things going today, Slimy?

Slimy Sam: Oh, things are a little slow today, baby. Seems like I've already swindled almost everyone out of their money. Sure wish some new folks would come to town, liven things up a bit.

Tiger Lily: Yea, I know what ya mean. This here's a real hick town.

(The curtain slowly closes)

(Then the curtain opens again for a final chorus of the song "Who Knows")

THE END

THE GREAT MUSICIAN

Once there was a little baby boy named Harry Macmillan. When he was six months old his parents bought him a toy trumpet. He started to play it. After about a minute or so he played the scale. His parents were amazed. So they bought him a music book when he was one.

When he was two he learned how to play "America the Beautiful." When he was old enough to talk he asked his parents if he could have a real trumpet and if he could get a trumpet teacher so he could play harder stuff. So on his fourth birthday he got a real trumpet. Then after a few weeks Harry went to his first trumpet lesson.

160

He had a nice teacher. His teacher's name was Mr. Portwood. After a year of lessons he was playing waltzes and stuff like that.

When he was six instead of going to regular school he went to trumpet school. In trumpet school they played the trumpet half of the school time and half was just like regular school.

When he got home from school all he would eat for supper would be an apple. He wouldn't eat because he was too busy playing his trumpet. Harry's parents were worried about him. They noticed that he was getting skinnier. So they took him to a doctor.

The doctor's name was Dr. Jekyll. "Well," said the doctor, "take the trumpet away from him and give it to him only when he goes to school."

So they tried it. Well, Harry would eat but when he ate an oatmeal cookie it would turn into oatmeal mush because his tears would go in his food. So they said they would give him his trumpet back if he promised to stop playing long enough to eat. So they tried it and it worked.

But in another year they had another problem. Harry got too good for Mr. Portwood. There was only one better teacher than Mr. Portwood and that person's name was Mr. Schwartz. But he charged $100 a week. "Please," said Harry, "I'll pay you back when I get thousands of dollars out of concerts and stuff."

So they decided to have Mr. Schwartz for a music teacher. But in a couple of years Harry got too good for Mr. Schwartz. So now Harry was the best musician in the world. When people heard about Harry they got all excited.

A concert hired him and a band hired him. He got ten million dollars for the concerts he played every month, and a million dollars every time he played in a parade. So he paid back his parents.

But in a couple of years something terrible happened. Harry was on his way down stairs, because the dressing room was downstairs and the concert was upstairs and he fell down the stairs and he broke two things: his trumpet and his leg.

Well, he just ruined his chances of going to one of the biggest concerts in the world. And his music teachers were going to be there. Well, his parents heard the noise and came to see what happened. When they saw him they took him to Dr. Lanion. Mr. Portwood and Mr. Schwartz came too.

161

"Well," said the doctor, "he won't be able to play his trumpet because he lost five of his permanent teeth." So when he got home Harry was very sad.

Mr. Portwood and Mr. Schwartz suggested that he should get false teeth. But Harry said that it was no use. He said that he would have to anyways every time he would blow his teeth would probably fall out.

Mr. Schwartz said maybe he could teach him to play without his teeth. But Harry said that it was no use. he said that he would have to find a job.

Well, you would think that after all those concerts that he'd have trillions and billions of dollars and wouldn't need a job, but the money went fast. Harry kept on buying better and better trumpets. Now, he only had fifty dollars.

Then Harry remembered that the gas station needed somebody to work there. Well, after ten years he was married and had eighteen kids. Now he was the boss of the gas station. And he had a very good life.

THE END

—Sandy White

THREE FOUND POEMS
by Regina

She pours the grain
from the basket to
separate the wheat
from the chaff.
The woman is
not beautiful,
but her sturdiness
is impressive.
She moves slowly
as she carries
her awkward,
heavy load
to the mill to
be processed.

At the end of
summer, harvesting
occupies her full energies.
The earth is
her provider.

The sailor at sea lives
in a world very
different from
the landlubber's.
Ship life has its
own character.
"She is stately,
noble, graceful,
majestic, and
gorgeous to behold,
the beauty of
them all."
Praise for a queen?
Almost,
It is praise for
a ship.
Everyone can feel
a tingle of
excitement when he sees
a ship.
A ship on the sea!
It makes us all
yearn for adventure,
for a different way of life.

The largest animal
of the world lives
in the sea.
If it were to
surround the
fisherman his
life would be lost.
Boats, too, have
a life cycle.

Boats must
be built.
Boats must
be repaired.
Boats are not
always at sea.

Summer
Flowers, bees and bugs
in the grass among the trees
summer's picture show.

Horses
Walk, trot and canter
Horses running like the wind
Racing the lightning.

New York City
Black, dirty buildings
Towering above the clouds
That's New York City.

Movies
Staring in horror
Watching a scary movie
Oh, how horrible.

Regina
Yelling and screaming
It's a famous movie star
Giving autographs

Leaves
Leaves sail with the wind
Green, orange, red and yellow
It's autumn once more

Flowers
Roses and daisies
Sweet smelling in summertime
In the green meadows

Air
Fast, slow, hot or cold
All sizes, shapes and colors
Air's the strangest thing.

Viet Nam
Shooting and bombing
What an awful sight to see
Why do they fight so

Clouds
Clouds float gently by
What a quiet, peaceful day
Look, a dog flew by.

A Storm
Lightning strikes the sky
Like whips whipping a bad world
The sun looks in scorn.

Stand alone
on a long
quiet beach
look out at
the ocean
everyone would
feel alone
but a Monk
would not miss
the importance
of such
a place
the prayerful
person with
the glory
and mystery
of Creation
Doesn't it seem
as if
the whole world

is there
around you
the earth and
the heavens
are all of
Creation?
Does the sky
have a limit?
Does the sea
have an end?
It might be
a feeling
of being
alone,
but not
necessarily
lonely.
Contemplation
comes more easily
to a monk
than to an
ordinary
person.
The expanse
of the seemingly
empty space
would have a
different
effect on
everyone.

THE GREEDY RIPOFF
(A play in seven scenes)
by John Durgin

SCENE I

(J. Paul Greedy is working in his office. It is a very fancy, all-electric office. Telephones are ringing, computers whirring and buzzing. Greedy is about eighty years old, and he just loves to press buttons)

Greedy: *(He writes a check, rips it out of the check book and puts it in an envelope. He is very efficient. The telephone rings.)*

J. Paul Greedy here. No, I don't care if Esso is changing its name. And I don't care what the Food and Drug Administration says about the TV commercial. So what if that truck is leaking oil.

(He hangs up. Phone rings again.)

Greedy here. What? Speak up, man. Greedy Shipping? Well, what do you want? You say we've taken too much oil from the sea? Well, how much is too much? Twelve million gallons? Well, dump it back. Use your head, man.

(He slams down the receiver. The phone rings again.)

Greedy here. Yes, by all means. Buy it right away. I don't care how much it costs, I said buy it. And get twenty thousand shares of Western Electric right away. And get rid of the Volvo shares, those Swedes don't know what they're doing.

(He slams down the receiver. The phone rings again.)

Greedy here. How's that again? *(Sweet & sarcastic)* You say Exxon is giving away thermal mugs? Wonderful, wonderful. Oh, and Sunoco is giving away football trading stamps? Good, good. And Shell is giving away hot wheels? That's very nice, very nice.

And now, let me understand you. You think that J. Paul Greedy should give away something, too. *(His voice changes back to a normal scream)* Listen to me you fool, you clown, you yellow-eyed bean. J. Paul Greedy gives away nothing—nothing. We, at Greedy Oil, take. We take and take and take. But we never give. You are fired.

(He hangs up, reaches for the intercom.)

167

Get me my lawyer!

*(There is a knock on the door. The lawyer comes in.
He is very slick and sophisticated. A playboy type.
Well dressed.)*

Lino: Yes, Mr. Greedy?

Greedy: *(Hardly looking up from his work.)* Oh, hello. What took you so long? There's an employee of mine who thinks we should give free handouts to our customers. I want you to make sure he is fired.

Lino: Yes, Mr. Greedy. I'll look into it right away. Anything else, Mr. Greedy?

Greedy: Yes, I have been informed that we are taking too much oil from the sea. Can this be correct? After all, we own most of the ocean, don't we?

Lino: Well, Mr. Greedy, we do own a good part of the Pacific.

Greedy: We?

Lino: I mean, of course, you own a lot of the Pacific. But there are a few other oil companies with interests in the Atlantic. Esso is big in the Atlantic, for example. I mean Exxon.

Greedy: Exxon, eh? Oh, yes, that's the company that is giving away those thermal mugs. Let me think. Hmmm. Make them an offer right away for the rest of the Atlantic.

Lino: Right away, Mr. Greedy.

Greedy: Oh, and Lino, I'm very busy today. My wife gets lonely waiting for me while I'm at work. Would you please do me the favor of taking her out to lunch?

Lino: Right away, Mr. Greedy.

(Lino leaves. Greedy works. Curtain.)

SCENE II

(A fancy chinese restaurant. Lino is pacing back and forth waiting for J. Paul Greedy's wife. He looks at his watch. He gets more and more nervous. Finally, Zelda comes flying in. They embrace.)

Zelda: Oh, Lino. It's been so long. How I have missed you. How desperate I have been.

Lino: Sh, Zelda. Not here. One of Greedy's men might see us. I

168

have reserved a table over there, in a secluded corner. Come, let me take your mink.

Zelda: *Oh, just toss it anywhere.*

(They go in and sit down. One other table on the stage is occupied by a single man in a dark suit wearing sunglasses. This man is really Charles, the Greedy Butler. He sits spying on the couple, writing down everything they say.)

Lino: *At last, my darling. We are finally alone.*

Zelda: *Lino, my dearest. We cannot go on meeting like this. J. Paul Greedy is sure to discover our romance. He will destroy us both. Oh, Lino, Lino, Lino, Lino, Lino! You must do something. Please Lino.*

Lino: *Zelda, I know. I have thought of a plot that I must discuss with you. But first, let us order.*

Zelda: *Yes, I'm so hungry I could eat a horse.*

Lino: *Waiter. Waiter. Over here please.*

Waiter: *Yes, sir. Man who sits in restaurant with beautiful dame has good game.*

Lino: *We'll start with a bottle of wine, please. Napoleon, 1932. It was a very good year.*

Waiter: *Yes, sir.*
Man who order 1932
know just what to do.

Lino: *(To Zelda) Where'd they get this crackpot! (To waiter) And after the wine, we'll have a double order of egg noodles and shrimp chow mein.*

Waiter: *Man who order shrimp chow mein*
never go insane.

Lino: *(Getting impatient) Yes, yes. And bring chop sticks, please.*

Waiter: *Yes, sir.*
Man who say please
always get the best from us Chinese. (He goes away)

Zelda: *Now darling, tell me, tell me!*

Lino: *I think I know how we can get rid of Greedy and keep all of his money at the same time. You know how nervous Greedy gets whenever he hears about these giveaway plans at other gas stations?*

Zelda: *Yes, he almost goes crazy whenever I mention Exxon thermal*

169

mugs, or Shell Hot Wheels....

Lino: Well, listen carefully. (Lino begins whispering just as the
           waiter comes back in.)

Waiter: Man who whispers in young girl's ear
           is welcome to eat here.

Lino: (To Zelda) Oh, no. He's back. I don't know what's happened
           to this restaurant. It used to be a good place. (To waiter)
           Listen, just serve the food, will ya?

Waiter: Yes, sir.
           But man who yell for food
           make for a very bad mood.

Lino: I don't care about the mood. I just wish that you would leave
           us alone. Now, we'd like to start with the chow mein.

Waiter: Yes, sir.
           Man who start with chow mein
           never go insane.

Lino: I heard that before. Now get on with it! Serve us our wine.

Waiter: Yes, sir.
           Man who wants 1932
           know just what to do.

Lino: Listen, bub. I'm going to proverb you if you don't shut up.
           Come on Zelda. Let's get out of here.

(They walk out. The waiter watches. Charles walks out. The waiter watches. Curtain.)

SCENE III

(Back at Greedy's office. At first no one is on stage. Then Greedy comes stomping in. He has a toy whistle in his hand. He slams the whistle down on his desk, then picks it up, looks at it furiously, and slams it down again.)

Greedy: (He picks up the phone.) You there. Get me my lawyer.

(He looks at the whistle again while waiting. His fingers are nervously tapping the table. Accidentally he blows the whistle. He jumps. Lino walks in.)

Lino: You wanted me, Mr. Greedy?

Greedy: Yes, I've been waiting. On the way to work this morning I
           stopped at one of my gas stations. I filled up the tank of my

170

| | limousine. *I was just about to drive away when the attendant came running out, and guess what happened?* |

Lino: *Why, I have no idea, Mr. Greedy. What happened?*

Greedy: *(Jumping out of his chair. Almost speechless with rage) The attendant gave me this...this thing ...this whistle. He gave it to me for nothing...free...free of charge. Can you imagine that?*

Lino: *Yes, Mr. Greedy. I can imagine that. All your gas stations have been giving away whistles all over the world ever since yesterday at four p.m.*

Greedy: *What? All my gas stations. You say they are all giving away whistles? For free? For nothing? Without cost? But why? Why? Why???*

Lino: *I was just following orders, Mr. Greedy. Don't you remember that you told me last week to find a product that we could give out at all our gas stations?*

Lino: *I mean, of course,* your *gas stations. So, I went to the Mattel toy makers and I bought 50 million crates of whistles.*

Greedy: *What? 50 million crates of whistles? You mean that I have paid for 50 million crates of whistles to give away? For nothing? But that's impossible. Listen to me you fool, you clown, you yellow-eyed bean. J. Paul Greedy gives away nothing. Nothing! We, at Greedy Oil, take. And take! And take!*

Lino: *But, Mr. G., I have your order right here. Let me read it to you. (Pulls an order slip from his pocket and begins to read.) Hmmm. Yes, it says right here—"My trusted friend Lino. We must begin to compete with Exxon, Sunoco and Shell. They are taking business away from us."*

Greedy: *What? Give me that! I could never have written that.*

(Lino hands over the order. Greedy examines it.)

Hmmm. That's my order, all right. I must have been suffering from exhaustion. I've been working too hard. Well, jolly good. I thought I told you never to give anything away to our customers, and I stand by that. So, since we've got the whistles, let's sell them. Put out a special order. From now on, anyone who purchases ten or more gallons of my gasoline, must also buy a whistle for five cents. If they don't buy the whistle, we'll slash their tires!

171

Lino: But, Mr. G., don't you think our customers will get angry with us?

Greedy: (Snaps) I'll make the decisions here. Now, what about that guy in shipping. Did you fire him?

Lino: Sir, you have been working too hard. Go home and take a break.

Greedy: Are you off your rocker or something? Don't forget. I've got a company to run. I can't take time off. Now, did you get rid of that crackpot down in shipping?

Lino: No. You said to make sure that he got a raise and a promotion to the Trucking Department. Why, I've got your order right here...(Reaches into his pocket)

Greedy: Never mind. Never mind. I'll take your word for it. Now get out of here. Leave me alone.

(Lino walks out. Greedy stares angrily at the wall. The phone rings.)

Greedy: Greedy here. Hmmm. Ummm. Hmmm. I see. Yes. You say that our gas is killing your car? That's impossible. Our gas comes direct from the ocean. It's the best refined gas around. What's that? You say you found a fish in your gas tank? Go ahead and get a lawyer. I've got the best lawyer around. Goodbye.

(He slams down the phone)

Oh, my head. Some day this has been. I'm losing my touch. I'm leaving.

(As Greedy is getting up from his desk, the phone rings again. He yanks the phone out from the wall.)

SCENE IV

(At the Greedy penthouse, Charles, the butler, is pacing nervously back and forth waiting for J. Paul Greedy's wife. He gets more and more nervous. Finally, Zelda comes flying in.)

Zelda: Oh, Charles. At last we're alone. It's been so long. How desperate I have been.

Charles: Shhh, Zelda. Not so loud. The maid might hear you. Come, let me take your mink.

Zelda: Oh, just toss it anywhere. Charles, how was I at the restau-

172

rant? Do you think that Lino believes that I love him? Do you think that he will betray Greedy?

Charles: You were wonderful, my darling. I didn't know you could act so well. You were really quite convincing. You'll soon have Lino following you around like a little puppy.

Zelda: Oh, if only it could be true. Soon we may actually control all of Greedy's gas stations. If only our plot works. And you know, Charles, don't you, no matter what I may say to Lino, I love only you.

Charles: Yes, Zelda, and I love you and will do anything for you.

Zelda: Kiss me, Charles.

Charles: Kiss me, Zelda.

(Greedy comes in)

Greedy: What a day I've had. Charles, get me my slippers.

Zelda: Greedy, you're home early.

Greedy: I know, I know. Don't remind me. Has the paper boy come yet?

Zelda: But Greedy, it's only four o'clock.

Greedy: Oh, swear, that's right too.

Zelda: Well, I'm going shopping. I'll stop and get a paper on my way back.

(Zelda puts on her fur stole and leaves. There's a knock on the door.)

Greedy: Come in.

(Lino comes in.)

Greedy: Oh, hello, Lino. You're just in time. Care to join me for a drink?

Lino: Don't mind if I do.

(Charles comes back in with a tray filled with drinks.)

Charles: Here you are, gentlemen. Triple Scotch on the rocks.

Lino: *(Gives Charles a strange look)* Haven't I seen you somewhere before?

Charles: Oh, no, sir. I'm sure not.

Greedy: Come, come, Lino. Let's have our drinks.

(Charles leaves)

Lino: I've got a court order for you. It's from a person you talked to on the phone. It seems he has a fish in his gas tank.

Greedy: Wait, wait. I've had enough problems for one day. Let's just drink off all our problems. Have some wine? Beer? Scotch? Anything you want.

(Much guzzling)

You know, Lino. Sometimes I think you're the only person around here that I can trust.

(Curtain)

SCENE V

(Back at the Chinese restaurant. Charles and Zelda enter together. They are both nervous. They walk to the same table used in Scene II. They sit down. The waiter appears.)

Waiter: *(To audience with a wink)* Woman with one man on each arm is sure to cause a lot of harm.

Charles: Oh, Zelda, that was close. Greedy nearly caught us back at the penthouse.

Zelda: You're right, Charles. That was a close one. We can't let ourselves become careless. After all, the fortune is nearly ours.

Charles: I don't know, Zelda. This is getting to be too much for me. Suppose Greedy discovers our plot. I just don't know if I can go through with it. Greedy likes me. He trusts me. How can I betray him?

Zelda: After all the work we've put into this thing, you'd quit now? I'd never speak to you again if you did.

Charles: But Zelda, I love you. Couldn't we just go off to South America together? Away from Greedy. We wouldn't be rich. But I am a good butler, and we could have a nice life together.

Zelda: Me? Run off with a butler? A poor servant? Don't you forget, I'm the wife of J. Paul Greedy. I'm used to having money. Lots of it. I thought you were the kind of man who wanted to succeed at any cost, even at the risk of imprisonment.

Charles: But Greedy does trust me. After all, I've been the chief butler for twenty years.

(The waiter returns. Clears his throat)

174

Zelda: You yellow-bellied sap sucker. I thought you really wanted to go through with this. Now I know what kind of person you really are. I'm leaving.

(The waiter clears his throat again. Holds out his order pad. Tries to get their attention)

Charles: No, Zelda. No! No! Don't leave me. I love you madly. You're the boss. I'll do anything you say.

Zelda: OK, that's more like it. You just remember that I'm the boss. Now, I've got it all figured out. Here's how we go on with our plot...

Waiter: *(Clears his throat—really loud)* Man with woman who's slow to order
must be the butler from across the border.

Charles: What? How did you know that I'm a butler from the British Isles? Who are you? What do you want?

Waiter: Waiter only cares about what you will eat
so he can get off his aching feet.

Charles: *(To waiter)* But where did you find out all these secrets?
(To Zelda) Where'd he find out these secrets?
(To waiter) Who are you?
(To Zelda) Who is he?
(To waiter) Are you a spy for Greedy?

Waiter: Man who think that I'm a spy
better look out that he may die.

Charles: Die! Spy! Schmy! Eye! Cry! This is ridiculous. Let's get out of here, Zelda.

Zelda: Yes, Charles, darling. Let's go somewhere else. It's too dangerous to talk about our plans here. Let's go to the Ritz.

Charles: *(Leaving)* Anywhere! Anywhere!

Waiter: *(Watches them go)* Man who leave an empty table
must not be very stable.

(Curtain)

175

SCENE VI

(Back at the Greedy office. At first no one is on stage. Then Greedy comes stomping in. He sits down at his desk looking very angry. Then slowly he reaches into his pocket and pulls out a bottle of soap bubbles. He examines it carefully. Opens it. Blows one bubble. Suddenly furious.)

Greedy: Get me my lawyer!

        (He paces nervously back and forth)

Lino: You wanted me, Mr. Greedy?

Greedy: What took you so long? Lino, listen. On the way to work this morning, it just happened that my limousine was a little low on Greedy Super Premium. I pulled into one of my New Jersey stations. I filled up, and I was just about to drive away when the attendant came running out, and guess what happened.

Lino: Why, I have no idea, Mr. Greedy. What happened?

Greedy: *(Jumping out of his chair, almost speechless with anger)* The attendant gave me this! This thing! These bubbles! Just take a look. He gave me this free of charge! Free, do you understand? Without charge! Do you understand?

Lino: Yes, Mr. Greedy. I understand. All your gas stations have been giving away Super-Bubble by Mattel to every customer since 12 midnight last night.

Greedy: What? What? All *my* gas stations? First you told me that I was giving away whistles. Now you tell me that I'm giving away Super-Bubble by Mattel. By why? Why? Why?

Lino: I was just following orders, Mr. Greedy. Don't you remember that you told me last week to order 50 million gallons of Super-Bubble by Mattel?

Greedy: No! No! I don't remember. You mean that I paid for fifty million gallons of Super-Bubble by Mattel? But that's impossible. Listen to me, you fool! You clown! You yellow-eyed bean! J. Paul Greedy gives away nothing. We, at Greedy Oil, take, and we take, and we take. Next thing I know you'll be showing me my order right in your pocket.

Lino: Of course, Mr. Greedy. I have it right here. *(Pulling order from his pocket)*

176

Greedy:	*(Staring at the order) But this is impossible. This is impossible. What do I want with all this Super-Bubble by Mattel? (He blows some bubbles. Really angry again) Get me my lawyer!*
Lino:	*I am your lawyer.*
Greedy:	*Swear. That's right too. But I'm J. Paul Greedy. I own most of the Atlantic, most of the Pacific, and more of the Indian than anyone else. I own gas stations all over the United States. Sunoco is afraid of me. Exxon is afraid of me. Everybody is afraid of me!*
	And why? Because I'm big. (He blows some more bubbles) Because I take, and take, and take. (More bubbles)
Lino:	*That's right, Mr. G.*
Greedy:	*That's right. That is right. That is right. I take and take and take. I never give. (Blows more bubbles)*

(The phone rings)

Greedy here. Oh, yes. The man with the fish in his gas tank. Well, that fish will cost you three dollars a pound. See my lawyer! (Hangs up phone. Blows more bubbles) We never give. We take and take and take and take. I'm King of Bubbles. I mean king of gas stations. I'm smarter than Gulf. I'm smarter than Shell, American, Pepco, Chevron and the rest. I'm the biggest and the best. (More bubbles)

Lino:	*That's right, Mr. Greedy. Whatever you say, Mr. G.*

(Phone)

Greedy:	*What? Who? Drilling for oil? Where? In China? We'll buy it! No, not the oil. The whole country. (Starts to hang up, then changes his mind) But don't buy any of those Chinese, send 'em to Russia. (He hangs up)*
Lino:	*Very good, Mr. Greedy.*
Greedy:	*You're right. I'm very good. I'm the king of them all. And I take and I take and I take and I take.... (Blows more bubbles, starts skipping around the table) and I take and I take and I take....*
Lino:	*That's right, Mr. G.*
Greedy:	*(Still skipping around, singing "I take and I take", etc.)*
Lino:	*(Sneaks over to the door, opens it and calls out) OK, boys, you can come in now.*

(Two men in white uniforms with Herbert's Funny Farm written on the back come in and grab Greedy. They carry him out.)

Greedy: *(Still singing) I take and I take and take...*

(They carry him out. At the last moment he seems to wake up a bit)

Lino! What is this? What's going on?

Men: *Shut up, you.*

(They leave)

Lino: *(Picks up the phone, dials) Hello, Zelda. The cat's in the bag. Meet you at the Chinese restaurant right away.*

SCENE VII

(Back at the Chinese restaurant. Lino is pacing nervously; Zelda comes flying in)

Zelda: *Lino, Lino. Is it true? Did they really take Greedy away?*

Lino: *Yes, Zelda, it's all true.*

(They embrace)

Zelda: *Oh, you wonderful man. I always knew you could do it.*

Lino: *Yes, Zelda. At last the Greedy gas stations are ours. All ours.*

Zelda: *Yes. They're all mine. Mine.*

Lino: *What?*

Waiter: *Man who comes into Chinese restaurant twice must like something besides fried rice.*

Lino: *Oh, no. Not you again. Come on, Zelda. Let's sit down.*

Zelda: *Oh, don't worry about him. Not at a time like this. (They sit) Oh, Lino, this is such a wonderful moment. After all our work, the Greedy fortune is mine. Now, of course, you've made out the necessary papers.*

Lino: *Yes, of course, Zelda. Here is the certificate from Herbert's Funny Farm certifying that Greedy is incurably insane.*

Zelda: *(Examines it) Good. Good. Good.*

Lino: *And here is the certificate certifying that we are now the proud owners of every Greedy gas station in the world.*

Zelda: *(Examines it) But, Lino, there is some mistake. The gas stations are mine.*

Lino: *But, Zelda, who did all the hard work? I did. Who put*

Greedy in the bag? I did. And you now say you own every gas station? What about me?

Zelda: Lino, Lino, my love. What's there to worry about? After all, I love you. Once we are married, we will share everything. I just want the certificate in my name.

Lino: Oh, Zelda, you are right. What difference does it make now we're together at last.

(He changes the certificates and hands them over to Zelda)

Zelda: *(Examines them)* That's better. Now, I am so hungry I could eat a horse. Let's order.

Lino: Good idea, Zelda. Waiter! Waiter! Waiter! Where is that idiot. He's always here when we don't want him.

(Lino turns around and looks back at Zelda. A Saturday night special is pointing in his face)

Zelda: See ya, Lino.

(Bam!) (Lino falls to the floor dead)

Waiter: Man with bullet in his head
surely must be very dead.

(The waiter drags Lino's corpse from the stage)

(Enter Charles. He paces nervously back and forth. Then notices that Zelda is already sitting at a table.)

Charles: Oh, Zelda, you're here early. Is everything alright?

Zelda: Yes, Charles, everything has been taken care of. Even Lino. Look here is a certificate saying that Greedy is insane. And this one says the fortune is all mine.

Charles: Oh, my Zelda!

Zelda: Oh, my Charles!

(They embrace)

Charles: This is a wonderful moment. Let's have a drink to celebrate. Waiter! Waiter!

(The waiter comes)

Bring us a bottle of wine, please. Chilled.

(The waiter gets the wine, turns his back on the table, and puts a fizzy in)

Waiter: *(Under his breath)* Man who drink this wine
Soon run out of time.

179

Charles: *Zelda, my darling. I have never known such happiness. Such...arragh...arragh (Gasp, grunt)*

(He falls to the floor)

Waiter: *Man who fall head first to floor*
Ain't in this play anymore.

Zelda: *At last, I'm free. (To the waiter) Did you pack our bags, darling? Did you get our tickets to the Iron Curtain, dear?*

Waiter: *Yes. Oldest Chinese proverb. She who get away from Greedy, better move fast, yes indeedy.*

(Curtain)

Teachers & Writers Publications

THE WHOLE WORD CATALOGUE 1 (72 pages) is a practical collection of assignments for stimulating student writing, designed for both elementary and secondary students. Activities designed as catalysts for classroom exercises include: personal writing, collective novels, diagram stories, fables, spoof and parodies, and language games. It also contains an annotated bibliography.

THE WHOLE WORD CATALOGUE 2 edited by Bill Zavatsky and Ron Padgett (350 pages). A completely new collection of writing and art ideas for the elementary, secondary, and college classroom. Deepens and widens the educational ground broken by our underground best seller, the first *Whole Word Catalogue.* Order two copies and get a free subscription for a friend.

IMAGINARY WORLDS (110 pages) originated from Richard Murphy's desire to find themes of sufficient breadth and interest to allow sustained, independent writing by students. Children invented their own Utopias of time and place, invented their own religions, new ways of fighting wars, different schools. They produced a great deal of extraordinary writing, much of it reprinted in the book.

A DAY DREAM I HAD AT NIGHT (120 pages) is a collection of oral literature from children who were not learning to read well or write competently or feel any real sense of satisfaction in school. The author, Roger Landrum, working in collaboration with two elementary school teachers, made class readers out of the children's own work.

FIVE TALES OF ADVENTURE (119 pages) is a new collection of short novels written by children at a Manhattan elementary school. The stories cover a wide range of styles and interests—a family mystery, an urban satire, a Himalayan adventure, a sci-fi spoof, and a tale of murder and retribution.

TEACHING AND WRITING POPULAR FICTION: HORROR, ADVENTURE, MYSTERY AND ROMANCE IN THE AMERICAN CLASSROOM by Karen Hubert (236 pages). A new step-by-step guide on using the different literary genres to help students to write, based on the author's intensive workshops conducted for Teachers & Writers in elementary and secondary schools. Ms. Hubert explores the psychological necessities of each genre and discusses the various ways of tailoring each one to individual students. Includes hundreds of "recipes" to be used as story starters, with an anthology of student work to show the exciting results possible.

JUST WRITING (104 pages) by Bill Bernhardt. A book of exercises designed to make the reader aware of all the necessary steps in the writing process. This book can be used as a do-it-yourself writing course. It is also an invaluable resource for writing teachers.

TO DEFEND A FORM (211 pages) by Ardis Kimzey. Tells the inside story of administering a poets-in-the-schools program. It is full of helpful procedures that will insure a smoothly running program. The book also contains many classroom-tested ideas to launch kids into poetry writing and an extensive bibliography of poetry anthologies and related material indispensable to anyone who teaches poetry.

BEING WITH CHILDREN, a book by Phillip Lopate, whose articles have appeared regularly in our magazine, is based on his work as project coordinator for Teachers & Writers Collaborative at P.S. 75 in Manhattan. Herb Kohl writes: "There is no other book that I know that combines the personal and the practical so well...." *Being With Children* is published by Doubleday at $7.95. It is available through Teachers & Writers Collaborative for $4.00. Paperback $1.95.

VERMONT DIARY (180 pages) by Marvin Hoffman. Describes the process of setting up a writing center within a rural elementary school. The book covers a two year period during which the author and several other teachers endeavor to build a unified curriculum based on the language arts.

THE POETRY CONNECTION by Nina Nyhart and Kinereth Gensler. This is a collection of adult and children's poetry with strategies to get students writing, an invaluable aid in the planning and execution of any poetry lesson.

TEACHERS & WRITERS Magazine, issued three times a year, draws together the experience and ideas of the writers and other artists who conduct T & W workshops in schools and community groups. A typical issue contains excerpts from the detailed work diaries and articles of the artists, along with the works of the students and outside contributions.

- -

☐ The Whole Word Catalogue 2 @ $6.95
☐ The Whole Word Catalogue 1 @ $4.00
☐ Teaching & Writing Popular Fiction @ $4.00
☐ Being With Children @ $4.00   ☐ $1.95 (Paper)
☐ Five Tales of Adventure @ $3.00 (10 copies or more @ $2.00)
☐ Imaginary Worlds @ $3.00
☐ A Day Dream I Had at Night @ $3.00
☐ Just Writing @ $4.00
☐ To Defend a Form @ $4.00
☐ Vermont Diary @ $4.00
☐ The Poetry Connection @ $4.00
☐ Subscription(s) to **T&W Magazine**, three issues $5.00, six issues $9.00, nine issues $12.00

NAME _____

ADDRESS_____

☐ Please make checks payable to Teachers & Writers Collaborative, and send to:
    Teachers & Writers   TOTAL
    84 Fifth Avenue   ENCLOSED
    New York City 10011 $_____